PITCH BLACK

ALSO BY ARTHUR BLACK

Basic Black
Back to Black
That Old Black Magic
Arthur! Arthur!
Black by Popular Demand
Blackmail! (with Lynne Raymond)
Black in the Saddle Again
Black Tie and Tales
Flash Black
Black & White and Read All Over

PITCH BLACK

Arthur Black

HARBOUR PUBLISHING

1 2 3 4 5 09 08 07 06 05

Published by
Harbour Publishing Co. Ltd.
P.O. Box 219
Madeira Park, BC
V0N 2H0
www.harbourpublishing.com

Edited by Susan Mayse
Cover and text design by Anna Comfort
Cover photography by Howard Fry
Printed and bound in Canada

Harbour Publishing acknowledges financial support from the Government of Canada through the Book Publishing Industry Development Program and the Canada Council for the Arts, and from the Province of British Columbia through the British Columbia Arts Council and the Book Publisher's Tax Credit through the Ministry of Provincial Revenue.

Library and Archives Canada Cataloguing in Publication

Black, Arthur
Pitch Black / Arthur Black.

ISBN 1-55017-367-7 / 978-1-55017-367-3

1. Canadian wit and humor (English) I. Title.

PS8553.L318P57 2005 C818'.5402 C2005-903203-0

ACKNOWLEDGEMENTS

Many thanks to *FiftyPlus* magazine, *Small Farms Canada* magazine, the *Victoria Times Colonist* and CBC Radio where some of these stories first saw the light of day.

CONTENTS

Introduction: On Being Out Of It 11

PART I: CANADEH

Saling, Saling 17
Where Have All the Icons Gone? 19
Coffee 22
Have a Nice Eh 25
Going to Pot 28
Danger! Hugs Ahead 31
On Being a Sex Object 33
Canada's Riviera: The Real Story 35
Heroes are Made, Not Born 38
It Takes a Thief 41
Canada: Too Small for Its Own Good 44
Let's Take the Turks! 47

PART II: BANANAS IN THE WILD

Confessions of a Carnivore 53
Anyone Heard from Chicken Little? 56
Danger! Teddy Bears Ahead 59
Have a Banana 62
Nothing Stuns Like a Deer 65
Feeling No Pain 68
Refugees Welcome, Pit Bulls Need Not Apply 71
Giving Geese the Bird 73
Don't Drink the H_2O! 75
Nessie: Missing and Presumed Dead 78
Friends, Romans, Countryskfxrlch 81

PART III: OF MICE AND MACHINES

The Phone-y War 87
It's All the Rage 90
Cycle Psychology 93
Dear Diary: You Make Me Sick 96
Hooray for Duct Tape—Warts and All 99
Come Fly with Me 102
Running on Empty 104
Karaoke? Okey-Dokey! 106
Measure for Measure 109
You Talking to *Me*, Toilet? 112
Keep it Simple, Stupid 115

PART IV: ONLY HUMAN

The War Between the Sexes 121
Of All the Nerve! 124
Warning! Kindness Ahead! 127
Watch Your Language! 130
Lotteries—You've Gotta Lotto Lose 133
Love Is Blonde 136
Name Your Poison 139
Nudes in the News 142
Earth to Prudes: Lighten Up 145
You Short? No Problem A-Tall 148
Down on the Farm—The Good Old Days 151
Just Call Me Unsuitable 154
Wheelbarrows and Chickens 157

PART V: PAINS AND PLEASURES

In Praise of Doing Nothing 163
Accustomed As I Am 166
Scrolled Any Good Books Lately? 169
Cars: Too Smart for Their Own Good 172
A Cross too Heavy to Bear 175
A Few Words About Facial Hair 178

This Won't Hurt A Bit 181
A Loaf of *Pane*, a Jug of *Vino Bianco* and Thou 184
The Simpsons? Fifteen? *Ay, Caramba*! 187
What Were They Thinking? 189
Food for Thought 192
We Didn't Get Sick 194
A Worm In Your Ear 197
In Praise of Praise 200

PART VI: PROMISES, PROMISES
How to Be a Rich and Famous Writer 205
Drugz 208
Fame Is the Name of the Game 211
Seemed Like a Great Idea at the Time 214
Down But Not Necessarily Out 217
I Hear Music 220
Never on Sunday 223
Advertising: The Not-Quite Exact Science 226
Where There's a Will 229
Gold Comfort 232

PART VII: WACKO WEIRDNESS
This is Your Lucky Day 237
The Circle Game 240
Of all the Crust! 243
Laugh? I thought I'd Diet 246
What's Your Phobia? 249
Elvis a Scot? Gude Laird! 252
Eye of Newt and Toe of Frog 255
It's a Fathead's World 258
Games People Play 261
Hair Today and Gone Tomorrow 264
The Madness of King George 267
Long Live the Tabs 270
Ideas: Dumb and Otherwise 273
Navel Intelligence 276

INTRODUCTION: ON BEING OUT OF IT

Well, well. Here I am, pecking out the first words of my eleventh book.

Wasn't supposed to work out like this, you know. I'm supposed to be sniffing roses full-time. I'm a retired guy. Turned in my front door key to the CBC building back in the spring of '02 after thirty years in the radio biz.

People still ask me why I packed it in, and I don't have a good answer, having held—after all—the best job in Canada. I was host of *Basic Black*, a weekly national radio show consisting of rare and quirky tunes blanket-stitched to interviews with the most oddball Canadians we could find.

I didn't have to interview politicians, movie stars or monosyllabic hip-hopsters. I had my own office, complete with a stuffed iguana on the filing cabinet and a black velvet Elvis portrait on the wall. I also had a staff of three, a free parking space in the heart of the city and periodic paid excursions to all corners of the country to do live shows in front of adoring fans. Workload? I was required to fill ninety minutes of air time once every seven days. Which meant that I sauntered into the office about noon on Wednesday and beat the weekend traffic by leaving just after lunch on Friday.

The job paid well, the dress code ran to Levi's and T-shirts and I got to share the water cooler with a raffish clutch of well-known Canucks like Shelagh Rogers, Bill Richardson, Jurgen Gothe—bright and amiable nutbars who are drawn to the CBC like fluffballs to the lint screen of a Maytag.

Best job in the country. And yet, and yet…

I just wasn't enjoying it anymore.

It was an Age Thing. When I started with the CBC, I was in my twenties. The music on the hit parade was my music—Moe Kaufman, the Beatles, the Stones. The country had a prime minister who canoed white water and slid down banisters. And I could skate faster than Wayne Gretzky (he was about seven at the time).

Then suddenly that prime minister was dead, as were half of the Beatles. And even the Great One was too old to keep up.

I too was having trouble keeping up. Not only did I not recognize the songs on the hit parade, I had never heard of the artists who performed them. I just assumed that Vanilla Ice was a dessert and Swollen Members was a porn flick.

And the radio business was changing. I was an obsolete hunt-and-peck typist awash in a tsunami of silicon-chip technology. I spurned the cellphone, avoided the pager, ignored the digital camera. I never figured out what a Palm Pilot or Blackberry actually did. The younger folks I worked with covered for me as best they could, but clearly something had to give.

My moment of truth: I'm reading the comic strip *Dagwood* in the *Globe and Mail.* Blondie is in a dress shop, uncertain the frock she's trying on looks good on her. "You look like Faith Hill," the sales rep tells Blondie. I pull my head out of the paper and ask the gang in the lunchroom, "Who's Faith Hill?"

My executive producer coughs defensively. Everyone else looks away.

Clearly I was drifting apart from my colleagues and my listeners. My mother ship—the Canadian Broadcasting Corporation—was chasing a two-to-thirty-nine-year-old audience demographic, and I was pushing sixty.

It was nobody's fault, but everyone around me was just getting too damned *young.*

So you can imagine my delight when I find a reader like you picking up my book. Suddenly I'm in the company of someone who remembers Ben Wicks, Marilyn Bell and Harold Ballard. Who knows what I'm talking about when I mention the Penticton Vees, *Front Page Challenge* or *The Happy Gang*.

Nice to be with you. Feels just like home. Okay if I put up my black velvet Elvis portrait?

PART I:
CANADEH

SALING, SALING

I guess it shouldn't be surprising that after I gave up being a mid-continent landlubber and moved to an island off the West Coast, I took up saling

Oh, not S-A-I-L-I-N-G, you understand. Ise not the bye who built de boat and Ise definitely not the bye who sailed her. My lone foray into the nautical world involved yours truly with his hand on the tiller, a fourteen-foot sailboat and an oversupply of hubris. It ended abruptly with the boat aground, my anchor missing and presumed drowned and me jackknifed over the sailing thwart partially mummified in the mainsail. No I'm not talking about that kind of sailing. I'm talking about S-A-L-I-N-G. Saling as in garage saling.

It's practically a blood sport on the island I call home because we really need garage sales here. See, we don't have Wal-Mart or Home Depot or Staples and frankly I think if they ever tried to open up on-island they'd starve to death. We don't do big box store shopping, and it costs at least twenty-seven bucks to take the ferry off-island and indulge. So mostly we don't. We stay home and do garage sales instead.

You might not think that an island of just a few hundred households could offer much in the way of garage sales on a weekly basis, but you'd be wrong. I don't know what it is about island living, but regular, ritualistic housecleaning seems to be a bigger deal here than other places I've lived. Maybe it's got to do with turning the page and starting a new life, but something kick-starts the garage sale bug on Salt Spring. Some folks I know have two, even three, garage sales a year. On the downside—you run across a lot of duplication. Don't forget that most islanders came from somewhere else. Usually somewhere chillier.

That's why you can almost always find mint-condition snow shovels, cross-country ski ensembles and tire chains still in their boxes. Not to mention thc ubiquitous fondue sets and Dan Hill CDs—a staple of garage sales everywhere in Canada.

Why the popularity of garage sales on the islands? Well, why not? When you think about it, where's the thrill in paying eighty bucks for a factory-fresh Tommy Hilfiger sweatshirt that looks exactly like everybody else's Tommy Hilfiger sweatshirt, when for five bucks I can pick up an already broken-in hand-knitted Cowichan sweater with a small but exclusive wine stain on the left sleeve?

We've all got enough stuff in our lives—but garage sale goodies offer stuff with soul. Split-cane fishing rods with the owner's initials burned into the hand grip…out-of-print Robertson Davies novels…slightly worn but utterly redeemable transistor radios and Pyrex bowls. These things all come with a past. They reek of history.

Actually the reek can be a little too pungent at times. I picked up a pair of gumboots for five bucks last month that still aren't allowed in the house.

But that's all right. Maybe they'll never get into the house. I'm okay with that too. Garage sale Zen. Either those gumboots will work their way into my life or they will transcend to another existential plane. Face their own personal karmageddon, as it were. On a plywood table at my own garage sale next spring.

For you—two bucks. Cheap.

WHERE HAVE ALL THE ICONS GONE?

Quiz time, folks. Your job is to suss out what the following folks have in common. Pamela Anderson. Alex Trebek. Neil Young. Mary Pickford. Jim Carrey. Leslie Nielsen. Michael J. Fox. Paul Anka. Conrad Black.

Well, yes, they are all media celebrities. Household names from Tallahassee to Tuktoyaktuk, but they are something else as well. They are all Canadians.

Or at least they used to be.

Now they are all Americans—with the exception of Lord Black, who flipped his Canadian passport over his shoulder in exchange for a British title and now, when nicked, bleeds only deepest Tory blue—except when he's hemorrhaging greenbacks.

The rest of the aforementioned ex-Canucks chose the Stars and Stripes as their flag of convenience—and they have various excuses for their switch. Neil Young was so disgusted with a Canadian audience's lukewarm reception at a concert that he stomped off the stage and straight into a US immigration office. He's been living in California ever since.

Hey, Neil—ever occur to you that maybe you were just, you know, *lousy* that night?

Alex Trebek came out of Sudbury, Ontario, cut his broadcasting teeth with CBC in Toronto, then packed his bags for Hollywood where he became the long-time host of the TV show "Jeopardy." He decided to dump his Canadian citizenship and become an American because "my wife is a Yankee and both my kids were born in the States."

Regina-born Leslie Nielsen discovered 'way back in the sixties that he could find much more work in the US film and TV industries than he could this side of the border. Adios, Canada.

Jim Carrey is even more enthusiastic. The plasticine-faced comic who grew up in the town of Newmarket, Ontario, positively gushes about his new-found land. "To me, this country [USA] defined me. This country allowed my dreams to come true."

All of the above offer different rationalizations for renouncing the land of their birth, but at bottom, the reason is the same right across the board.

Money. Call it more opportunity, fresh horizons, bigger audiences, more generous contracts—call it what you like. It all boils down to fatter wallets for those who go south.

Which I guess is as good a reason as any to forsake your birthplace. After all, most Canadians are here because at some point in history our forebears in Cracow or Aberdeen or Naples or Düsseldorf decided the Old Country was played out and the grass looked greener in that vaulting, mammoth far-off land called Canada. This country would not exist were it not for brave souls who were willing to trade in their heritage for a fresh start.

So why do I not feel admiration for the Jim Carreys and the Pamela Andersons, the Leslie Nielsens and the Alex Trebeks?

Partly because I know they weren't really desperate. They would have done fine here in Canada. They just wanted more.

And partly it's because I don't know how it's possible to cease to be what you are. How do you stop being a Canadian?

The writer Robertson Davies said it best. "I just am a Canadian," he told a reporter. "It's not a thing you can escape from. It is like having blue eyes."

Some cross-border Canadians obviously don't agree. I have an old pal who makes a tenuous living as a writer in Hollywood. From time to time he phones and updates me on celebrity sightings, backstage gossip and his latest writing coups. Last time he called I sensed something different in his voice.

"You sound funny," I told him. "You got a cold or something?"

"Actually," he said, "I'm taking a language pronunciation course. I'm trying to lose my Canadian accent."

The guy's not an actor. Why would he worry about a Canadian accent?

Besides, a Canadian accent can launch a career. Look what it did for Jeff Douglas, the guy that played Joe in the Molson beer commercial. You know the one—the "I am Canadian" rant?

Yeah, well. Jeff Douglas doesn't live here anymore. He moved to Los Angeles last year. More opportunities, he says.

Maybe he's right. The beer he was advertising—Molson Canadian—is now a wholly owned subsidiary of the American giant Coors.

Would the last Canuck to leave please turn out the lights?

COFFEE

You know why most people never move to the Gulf Islands? The economy. Sure. Once you've made the decision, quit your mainland job, hopped the ferry with all your worldly goods crammed into the trunk and strapped onto the roof of your Chevy Nova—once you're on the island, what are you going to do? To support yourself, I mean?

Oh, it's no problem for the dot-com gazillionaires, the semi-retired rock stars and the superannuated Calgary oil executives—but that's about 0.0014 percent of the population. What about the rest of us?

The Gulf Islands are not Silicon Valley. There are no auto plants or pulp mills on Texada or Denman. No Wall or Bay or Howe Street financial districts. We don't even have big box stores or McDonald's.

So what does an average Gulf Islander do to put in his or her time? I can answer that. We drink coffee.

Drinking coffee is unquestionably the prime Gulf Islands pastime, certainly on Salt Spring, where I live.

Mind you, I'm using the term "coffee" loosely here. Individual Salt Springers may drink cappuccinos, soy lattes, Americanos or powdered Nesçafé in a Dixie cup. They may also opt for jasmine tea, Walla Walla blend organic betel chai, steamed Mango Essence Surprise or Mother

Parkers Instant...but one way or another, Gulf Islanders spend an inordinate amount of time sitting around sucking hottish caffeinated liquids out of cups.

Which makes the slurp industry about as close to a big business as the Gulf Islands get. Not long after I landed here, I heard that some acquaintances were planning to open a new coffee shop downtown. Now my name's Arthur, not Conrad. I don't pretend to have a lot of business sense. But even I, financial nincompoop that I am, recognize a doomed flight of kamikaze commerce when I trip over it. These folks were about to commit economic suicide.

They planned to open a coffee house about fifty feet from Barb's Buns, a very popular watering hole, and fifty feet in the other direction from a place called Moka House—also a major hangout for island caffeine freaks. Plus the new establishment would be less than a sugar cube toss from at least a half-dozen other cafés, bistros, diners and beaneries—all of which already served a more than decent cuppa java.

Were they nuts? No question. Did they listen to my warnings? No. They went right ahead and opened a place called Roasters. And today? Well, today—if you go in really early—you might get a seat at Roasters. If you leave it too late, you'll join the tail of the takeout line snaking out the back door.

Roasters fared so poorly that pretty soon they opened another Roasters at the far end of the island. Which gave them the same number of Salt Spring outlets as Canada Post. And twice as many as the local constabulary.

So coffee houses are big business on the islands, but the fact is that most of us are not cut out to be coffee shop owners. We don't fly that high. Our job is to hold up the other end of the caffeine equation—namely to drink the product.

And I'm not pretending that it's an easy or lucrative way to spend your life. This is no nine-to-five, union-padded gig we're talking about here. Coffee drinkers don't get covered under any special dental plan or extended health benefit scheme. The hours are brutal, and we don't get six-week vacations or a chance to buy shares in the company. The lowliest sales peon in the backwardest used car lot in the province gets a desk, a phone, a computer and all the paper clips he can lift. In my line of work, you're lucky if you get a coffee card.

I'm not complaining. I'm merely pointing out that caffeine is to the Gulf Islands as crude oil is to Alberta. It's the lifeblood that makes this economy work.

And we coffee drinkers, we're the spud men and the roughnecks that get that caffeine out of the espresso machines and into the public bloodstream where it belongs.

So no fanfare—we don't expect that. But a little respect would be nice. Next time you see a professional coffee drinker hunched over his or her double soy macchiato…a little smile…perhaps even a casual salute. They're ruining their kidneys for you. In the immortal words of Churchill (that would be Randolph, not Winston), "They also serve who only slouch and slurp."

HAVE A NICE EH

In his book *Colombo's Canadian References*, John Robert Colombo defines *eh*? as "a colloquial expression meaning "What did you say?""

Mr. Colombo is correct, as far as he goes—but that's not nearly far enough. As any card-carrying Canuck can attest, *eh* is much more than a monosyllabic request for repetition or clarification. *Eh* is the primary Lego block of Canadian slang. In some parts of the country, *eh* festoons casual conversation like blueberries on a hillside. "So I was walkin' down the trail, eh? And suddenly there's this moose, eh? Well, I only got the four-ten with me, eh? So ennyways I drops back, eh? And..."

And so on. The popular conception is that *eh* is purest Hoserspeak. A redneck affliction restricted to taverns, bingo halls, hockey arenas, fish camps and other hick hangouts where guys in plaid jackets wearing ball caps over their mullets tend to congregate to drink beer from the bottle and converse in monosyllables.

Not true. I have heard the word *eh* tumble from the lips of professors, police officers and politicians. The only thing the speakers had in common was their passport. *Eh* is nothing if not egalitarian.

Other tongues have linguistic crutches that are something like our *eh*. The French cobble a *n'est-ce pas* onto many of their sentences. The Spanish throw in superfluous *si*'s and *verdads*. Germans often tack on a *ja* to flesh out a statement. Americans fall back on *huh*, as in, "Weird weather we're having, huh?"

But none of them are quite as elastic or ubiquitous as the good ol' Canadian *eh*.

Not that it gets any respect. The British writer-fop Quentin Crisp was appalled when, on his first trip to Canada, a Customs and Immigration official at the Toronto airport stamped his passport, looked up with a cheery grin and said, "Vindicated at last, eh?"

"You're too kind," Crisp muttered witheringly and moved on. Later he wrote about the *eh* phenomenon, calling it "a species of linguistic dim-witticism to which Canadians are addicted."

Well, how can we plead but guilty as charged, eh? The expression is as Canadian as back bacon, maple syrup, GST and Rocket Richard, right?

Wrong. Turns out that the word is cosmopolitan and cross-cultural and goes all the way back to the Middle Ages. It was popular enough by 1773 for Oliver Goldsmith to use it in his play *She Stoops to Conquer*. In 1851 Herman Melville thought so highly of what my Oxford English Dictionary grandly defines as the "interjectional interrogative particle often inviting assent to the sentiment expressed" that he threw it into *Moby Dick*.

Eighteen times.

"But flukes! Man, what makes thee want to go whaling, eh?"

Still, if *eh* wasn't born in Canada, it certain took out Canadian citizenship papers as soon as it washed ashore. A recent survey of first-year University of Toronto students reveals some intriguing commonalities. Asked to name distinctive Canadian things, the kids cited hockey, the maple leaf flag, our currency, peacekeeping, Canadian beer…

And *eh*.

Ninety-four percent of the university students said they were familiar with—and generally fond of—the expression, even though they admitted using it was something less than high-class.

Elaine Gold, who conducted the survey recalls, "One of the students' comments was so cute. He said, 'I was kind of proud when it slipped out of my mouth for the first time.'"

Gold said, "They're very aware of it and do see it as Canadian."

Me too. *Eh* may not be elegant, but it's as hardy as a beaver's incisor and as handy as a Robertson screwdriver (also Canadian). *Eh* is something you stand a very good chance of hearing shoehorned into any conversation from Tuktoyaktuk to Trois Rivières, from the Queen Charlottes to Come By Chance.

And if you're a Canadian who considers that fact to be bush league, low-class and altogether hard to accept, I can only offer the advice proffered by those stalwart Canadian icons, the brothers McKenzie: Bob and Doug.

Take off, eh?

GOING TO POT

Did I ever tell you about the time I impersonated a cop?

Relax, sergeant—it was several years ago, in another provincial jurisdiction. I lived in the sticks at the time, the hour hand had long passed midnight and some party-hearties in a house down the road were making noise. Way too much noise.

I took it for an hour and a half and then I called the cops. A bored dispatcher informed me that, as it was the weekend and due to budgetary cutbacks, no police were actually on duty, but an officer could be summoned from a nearby jurisdiction "in an extreme emergency."

I was younger then, with a shorter fuse and not nearly the level of urbanity and decorum for which I am so justly renowned today. Accordingly, I slammed down the receiver, said some bad words, put on my police hat and loaded my police dog into my cruiser. Together we drove down the road and fetched up in the driveway of the aforementioned party house.

A word about my cruiser, my police hat and my police dog.

The "cruiser" was an '82 white Ford station wagon. Something Ned Flanders might drive. The police hat was a nylon mesh cap I picked up after a charity softball game between a rural police detachment and the radio station I worked for. (Over a post-game beer, the cop who played shortstop informed me he coveted my CBC ball cap. We swapped.) The crest on the front of my new cap read "Ontario Provincial Police, South Porcupine." Not exactly a slogan calculated to strike fear into the hearts of evildoers, but a collector's item, I felt.

My "police dog" Rufus was in truth a mangy border-collie-and-indeterminate-mix mutt, but I hoped that in the dark and from a distance he might pass for an on-duty Alsatian.

I hammered on the front door, which was ajar, walked in, and in my best Lorne Greene voice of doom boomed, "WE'VE HAD SEVERAL COMPLAINTS ABOUT THE NOISE YOU PEOPLE ARE MAKING. IF YOU CAN'T TONE IT DOWN, I'M GONNA HAVE TO LAY CHARGES."

What I did was totally illegal, not to mention surpassingly stupid. But it worked like a charm. Know why?

Because it was a pot party, not a booze party. The joint reeked of...well, joints. And as I delivered my sermon, people all over the room were surreptitiously divesting themselves of baggies, stubbing out roaches, palming ashtrays and trying desperately not to exhale in my face.

What's more, they were all stoned. Instead of seeing me as the ridiculous impostor I clearly was, they were figuring that the dope they were smoking was unusually excellent.

Know what would have happened if that had been a booze party instead of grass fest? There's a good chance I would have been stomped into a carpet stain. And I'm not exaggerating. That very fate befell a lawyer in Squamish, BC, not long ago. He went to a booze party at a neighbour's house to ask people to pipe down. Two of the knuckle-dragging juiceheads in attendance kicked him to death.

All of which is a long-winded way of getting to my point, which is: why the hypocrisy about marijuana?

Recently, the federal New Democrats did backflips to distance themselves from their leader Jack Layton's rather brave endorsement of the substance. Politicos of other stripes (yellow) puffed themselves up to solemnly intone how they'd never touched the stuff—and who can forget Bill Clinton's pathetic cavil: "I smoked, but I didn't inhale"?

Well, I did, Bill—and what's more, I don't know of more than half a dozen adults who haven't tried pot at least once. It's no big deal, folks. Let's finally admit it.

Am I advocating pot for everyone? No. I don't smoke it anymore because it's too expensive, not worth the hassle and it makes me stupid. It also makes me hungry and lazy—two conditions I have enough trouble grappling with when I'm clear-headed.

All I'm saying is, let's stop being two-faced about it. Booze causes a thousand times the grief, bloodshed and property damage that pot does, but we turn a blind eye because through a fluke of justice and thanks to the twisted principles of seedy old perverts like J. Edgar Hoover and Alberta's own Emily Murphy, alcohol is legal and marijuana isn't.

The Canadian legal system is woozily staggering toward righting this absurdity, but it's not there yet, so think twice or even three times before you flout the law, even if the law is, to paraphrase Dickens, a demonstrable ass when it comes to a backyard weed.

But if you must smoke—keep it down. Don't make me put on my police hat and come over and bust you.

DANGER! HUGS AHEAD

Well, I've been living in the Gulf Islands for ten years now—which doesn't exactly give me bragging rights, but it does put me in a position to offer a cultural observation or two.

Such as: What's the big deal, anyway? What's so different about living on Pender Island compared to Penticton? Cranbrook compared to Galiano? Sicamous compared to Salt Spring? If somebody blindfolded you and dropped you off in, say, downtown Ganges—how would you even know you were on a Gulf Island?

Well, it's very simple. If you are on a Gulf Island, sooner—rather than later—someone will come up and hug you.

Don't ask me why. I spent most of my life ricocheting across Canada, getting by on nods, winks, waves and handshakes—and not being hugged all that much, aside from close family and (all too rarely) consenting members of the opposite sex.

But the very first person I met when I got to Salt Spring wrapped me in a big, smothering bear hug.

And he was my real estate agent.

And we're not talking that fake Hollywood kiss-kiss, squeeze-squeeze fabulous dahling, microhug, no. Gulf Islands hugs are heartfelt, wholesome, solemn and...long-ish. Your Gulf Islands hug can last longer than a Todd Bertuzzi cross-checking minor.

The classic Gulf Islands hug, which is as formal and ritualistic as a coronation at Westminster Abbey, goes like this. Hugger and huggee advance toward each other until they are deeply into each other's personal space. Beatific smiles, though not mandatory, are recommended. Both parties slowly throw arms wide and glide in for the clinch. As full frontal contact is made, all four arms close rapturously in maximum hug mode while, simultaneously, each party's chin goes over the other's right shoulder. Eyes should be closed at this point. If beatific smile is not in place, a look of intense bliss is acceptable.

This pose is maintained in total, ecstatic silence for minimum thirty seconds, after which both parties smoothly swivel heads backward and to the right, bringing chins to rest on each other's left shoulder. Hold and marinate meaningfully for at least half a minute.

This is the formal conclusion of the Gulf Islands hug.

Both parties can now step back and speak normally. "Hey, Kevin, how's it goin', eh? D'ja get your garage shingled yet?"

Needless to say this is all deeply bewildering for most visitors to the Gulf Islands—and for some islanders too. Like me. I'm of Scottish ancestry. We don't hug. Not without a lot of...well, Scotch.

But, that's the way it is—and it could be worse. Last summer we had a guy came back to the island after spending five years in LA. He was Mr. Cool. With the diamond earring. The white linen jacket. The Converse sneakers with no socks.

He was sashaying down the bar at Moby's giving high fives to everybody, slapping palms. Doing that hippy-dippy thumb-clutch thing where you grab the other guy's thumb and kinda saw back and forth like you're bucking up firewood...When he got to me, he put out his fists for that ultrahip fist-bump that morphs into a game of one potato, two potato. But I was too fast for him. Quick as a flash, I grabbed him in a bear hug and held him 'til he came to his senses.

Cruel? Hell no. My turf, my rules. Come to the Gulf Islands, you're gonna get hugged. It's the law.

ON BEING A SEX OBJECT

This is a heartfelt apology to Janet Jackson. Janet, I had no idea. Oh, I was one of the nattering nabobs, one of the press jackals who mocked and derided what became known as your "wardrobe malfunction" during the halftime entertainment for Super Bowl XXXVIII.

For any listeners who were adrift at sea, trapped in a coal mine or visiting Venus during that Super Bowl, I should explain that during Janet's act, her right breast was briefly exposed, subjecting unprepared viewers to the brief and ghastly sight of—there's no pleasant way to say this—a human nipple.

Naturally, chaos ensued. A continent reeled in shock and disbelief. The US Federal Communications Commission slammed the offending network, CBS, with a $550,000 fine for allowing the outrage to air. More than a half a million US dollars. Did they realize it would take CBS nearly 7.5 seconds of Super Bowl advertising revenue to make that money back?

But network hardship is not my point here. My point here is that I was scathingly cynical about Janet Jackson's part in what I viewed as the so-called accident. Until I too became a victim of sexual exploitation.

This happened not long after I became a sex object myself. Last month, when I became involved with something called the Maid on Salt Spring calendar project. It's a fundraiser inspired by an organization called Copper Kettle, which is trying to help homeless folks on the island. I, along with eleven other Salt Spring hunks of simmering sensuality, agreed to appear—as a sexpot, I guess—on a calendar called Maid on Salt Spring. I was—and please try to contain yourself as you read these words—Mr. July. Oh, and about that "maid" in "Maid on Salt Spring"? It's spelled M-A-I-D for a reason. Because all twelve participants are dressed in the same apparel. To wit: a French maid's costume.

Which is to say a wispy piece of black see-through frou-frou fringed in white lace. My photo—that is, Mr. July's—shows a winsome creature languidly reclining on a couch, feather duster at hand, with a rakish décolletage showing—and here's where the Janet Jackson connection strikes—showing a swatch of hirsute right breast right down to—and there's no mistaking it friends—the purplish hue of a...you know...the N-word.

Or it used to show. I saw the digital photo, folks. The nipple was there, front and centre. But somewhere between photograph and printed calendar some sharp-eyed Copper Kettle Keeper of All That's Good and Decent spotted the errant conical eminence surmounting my defunct, default mammary gland and ordered the printers to excise same from the final product. Which is why I appear in the Maid on Salt Spring calendar, smiling and relaxed despite my obvious nipple-lessness.

Could have been worse. Arvid Chalmers, a local comedian, musician and real estate legend, had his—dare I say—ample cleavage airbrushed into oblivion. Arvid—a.k.a. Mr. April—looks...winsome enough...for a man in drag. Except for the apparent massive scar tissue between his left and right breasts.

But you know the old expression about not seeing the forest for the trees? I think the feckless fault-finders of the Copper Kettle calendar calibrated their traps too fine. Oh, they snagged my nipple, and sandbagged Arvid's cleavage...but check out Mr. May, otherwise known as Valdy.

I'm pretty sure Valdy isn't wearing any underwear.

CANADA'S RIVIERA: THE REAL STORY

A poignant letter to the editor appeared in the *Victoria Times Colonist* recently from a reader back east in Markham, Ontario. I know Markham. I used to live near the town. Near enough to share its winters, anyway. Which is to say a yearly dose of four months of snow, sleet, hail, black ice and bone-chilling cold. That's kind of what this letter is about. It begins, "It's starting again—the clipped newspaper cartoons that depict freezing Easterners digging out of five-foot snowbanks while Vancouver Island folk bask in heat waves and bloom counts.

"These cartoons start showing up in my mailbox beginning in September. The bombardment continues until late spring. They come from so-called 'friends' on Vancouver Island. Do you people have any heart at all? This constant gloating and rubbing salt in our freezing wounds is really too much!" The letter's signed Jane Bargout, Markham, Ontario.

Well, Jane, you probably can't stop West Coast weather smugness, but you can fight back, and I've got just the eighty-seven-page antidote in my chubby little fist. It's a book—a broadside really—called *Rain and Suffering: The Real Gulf Islands Guide*, by Steven Grayson. Anybody who knows Gulf Islanders knows that when it comes to weather gloating, we are the smuggest of the smug. Haughtier than Vancouverites.

Even more condescending than Victorians. At least we were until this was published.

The introduction sets the tone: *"There are many beautiful guidebooks to the Gulf Islands. This is not one of them. An overzealous travel industry with neither shame nor morals has created the myth that the Gulf Islands are a paradise waiting to be discovered. This myth is perpetuated by lying tourists who stayed here and are now too proud to admit their mistake... The Gulf Islands are part of the Canadian dream of having some place in our country like Hawaii...*

"It's one thing to dream. It's another thing to believe that hanging off the edge of Canada, at a latitude closer to Alaska than the equator is some balmy paradise that doesn't require a passport."

The book also has warnings about interacting with Gulf Islanders. Grayson describes the denizens as *"a desperate people, who left the mainland one step ahead of the law and who had such poor geographic skills they didn't realize they hadn't landed on Vancouver Island. They consider everyone a possible informant who might recognize them from their former lives. Do not make eye contact. Keep in mind that these people can't remember the last time they were warm or dry. Rain has been hitting them on the head for eleven and a half months every year since they got here. They have no sense of humour and even less sense of fun. If caught between a cougar and an islander, walk slowly toward the cougar."*

Grayson manages to leave not one aspect of Gulf Islands life unpummelled. Listen to him cross-check Gulf Islands climate, economy and residents in one sentence: *"Islanders pride themselves on not letting the rain deter them from their usual duties, which consist of working at jobs they hate so they can buy more things to repair their houses so the rain floods in a little less."*

No island escapes Grayson's wrath. Gabriola? *"A sausage-shaped retirement community rumoured to rise six to eight feet every week when its senior citizens catch the 9:00 a.m. ferry to go shopping in Nanaimo."*

Lasqueti? *"Since there is no electricity on the island, most of the residents have been driven mad by the sound of their neighbours' gasoline generators."*

Salt Spring? *"Considered one of the most miserable of the Gulf Islands; the inhabitants can't even agree if the name of the island is one word or two."*

Well, I guess Steve Grayson would know about that, because he lives on Salt Spring Island where, when he's not blowing holes in the Gulf Islands myth, he grows and sells...organic walnuts. How Gulf Islands can you get?

Do his fellow Salt Springers hold a grudge against Grayson for writing a book that lays bare all our flaws? Of course not. We're open-minded. Thick-skinned. As a matter of fact, the Salt Spring Chamber of Commerce is sponsoring a book launch party for Steve this weekend. We're all invited to come and get behind Steve and his new book.

The invitation says all we have to bring is feathers. The Chamber will supply the tar.

HEROES ARE MADE, NOT BORN

Heroes come in different shapes and sizes and they come to us by different delivery systems. Mario Lemieux arrives on skates. Rick Hansen rolls up in a wheelchair. Roberta Bondar shows up with an astronaut helmet under her arm. Silken Laumann glides to the dock in a sleek racing shell, her hands on the oars.

Then there's Mary Helen Moes. She appears in your email inbox and wants to know what you're going to do to help her Emergency Paediatric Campaign (EPC). She's never played in the NHL and doesn't use a wheelchair. She's not an Olympic celeb like Silken, nor has she orbited the planet like Roberta. She's a shy suburban housewife with three kids and a dog. She's a different kind of hero.

Mary Helen Moes lives in Peterborough, Ontario. She grew up in the area along with five other kids.

One of whom almost didn't. Twenty years ago, her brother was born with only one-quarter of a kidney and a blocked bladder. Medical technology being what it is, the boy was saved and eventually grew to be a healthy adult.

And Canada's tattered and threadbare health care system being what it is, Mary Helen Moes's parents were ruined in the process. It wasn't the cost of the surgeries that did them in—that was covered. No, it was the unexpected expenses. The medical expertise was far away in Toronto. The countless trips to the city and long recuperations in hospitals meant expensive stays in city hotels and pricey restaurant meals, not to mention precious time away from a working dairy operation.

Mary Helen's brother needed dozens of operations. The experience sucked up every penny the family had saved—and all they could borrow. By the time Mary Helen's brother was eight years old and healthy, his parents had lost their dairy farm.

Watching one's parents go through an ordeal like that could crush a person and shatter her will.

Or not.

Mary Helen Moes pretty much put the nightmare behind her until, watching Oprah one day, she learned of a program in the United States that helped American parents of children facing extended hospital stays. A bell rang in the back of her head. She remembered what it was like, watching the family cows being loaded onto a truck and shipped away. She wondered if there was any comparable program in her area to help out parents of stricken kids. She made a few phone calls. There wasn't. She asked health care experts if they could use such a program.

Sure could.

Nobody talks about it much, but if you add up all the expenses that parents or guardians face when they have to stay with ill children who are being treated at centres away from home—the meals, the accommodation, the gas, the babysitters, not to mention the lost wages—it comes to about ten thousand dollars over three months. Ronald McDonald House in Toronto helps people in need—but even it dings you twenty dollars a night. That's a hundred and forty bucks a week. And you can't wave your health care card to make it go away.

So Mary Helen Moes decided to create what she called the Emergency Paediatric Campaign. She made the rounds of local businesses, trying to drum up money. She called up radio talk shows. She wangled interviews with local newspapers.

Understand that Mary Helen Moes had no experience at any of this. She knew from diddly about public relations, fundraising, health service liaison or any of the nuances of running a sophisticated public service.

She just did it.

One mother, Stacey Bondy, remembers what it was like when her newborn son came into the world with five holes in his heart.

"He didn't come home for a month," she recalls. Stacey and her mother stayed at the hospital virtually day and night. "It makes you crazy," she says. Then someone told her about the EPC. The Bondys phoned to see if they qualified for help.

"Mrs. Moes just came right up to the room after his surgery and handed us money," says Stacey. She also brought advice and encouragement. She knew what Stacey was going through. She'd been there.

So far, the campaign has helped more than seventy families facing the nightmare of nursing a child through a critical illness in faraway hospitals. And it's all thanks to one woman who didn't want other families to go through what her family suffered.

Funny thing about heroes—they're not always larger than life. Sometimes they look just like your next-door neighbour. Like Mary Helen Moes. Will Rogers once said, "We can't all be heroes, because somebody has to sit on the curb and clap as they go by."

Put your hands together for Mary Helen Moes.

IT TAKES A THIEF

Don't it always seem to go
That you don't know what you got 'til it's gone...
—Joni Mitchell

There's a thief in the neighbourhood.

A chilling six-pack of words, that—but true, alas, of my neighbourhood—which is not, I hasten to add, downtown Baghdad or the Lower Bronx. Not even Yonge and Dundas in Toronto or East Hastings Street in Vancouver. I live in a tame and quiet little corner of Canadian countryside five miles from the nearest streetlight with nary a high-rise to blight my horizon. It's a place where everybody knows everybody else, along with their kids, their dogs and the kind of cars they drive. We have no bars, no casinos, no strip joints—not even a gas station or a 7-Eleven. Our neighbourhood is not, in short, what you'd call a fecund petri dish for a one-man crime wavelet, but it seems we've got one just the same.

He's a weird specimen, our thief. (I'm assuming it's a he because most thieves—most crooks, in fact—are male. As some wiseguy once said, "The race is not always to the swift, but that's the way to bet.")

So far our thief has stolen a hundred bucks out of a wallet, but left the credit cards intact. He's also lifted another neighbour's Palm Pilot and his global positioning device but ignored a fat billfold sitting right next to them. In his only break-and-enter, the thief busted a window to get into a vacant house, used the coffee machine (?!?) and then left, taking—as far as anyone can tell—nothing more than a bellyful of java.

Naturally the police were notified. In due course a constable rolled up in a cruiser and started asking the standard questions and taking notes. This house where the gizmos were stolen—it was locked, right? Well...no, not really. And the wallet that the money was stolen from, where was that? Umm, it was sitting on the dashboard of a pickup parked by the road. But the pickup was locked, right? Actually...no. As a matter of fact, the keys were in the ignition, too.

I couldn't see the cop's eyes, but I'm pretty sure they were rolling back in his head. Who could blame him? He's got a tough enough job without playing nursemaid to a gaggle of gormless burghers who practically have *rob me* signs Scotch-taped to their foreheads. He probably thought we were idiots, but he was nice enough not to let it show. He told us the thief sounded too dumb to be professional. Probably a druggie. He advised us to be aware of any strangers lurking in the neighbourhood.

"Oh, and lock your doors from now on," he added, resisting, no doubt, the urge to add "ya morons."

The cop was right, but he was wrong as well. We didn't leave our doors unlocked because we're stupid; we left them unlocked because we *could*. That's the kind of neighbourhood we are—or were. If you were going to Mexico for a week or two, well sure, you locked up and notified your neighbours. Other times, why bother?

All that's changed now. There's a new sense of vigilance in the neighbourhood. We no longer assume that cars rolling through our streets are rubbernecking tourists or folks just out for a drive. A kid with a skateboard under his arm walking down the road is no longer just a kid with a skateboard. Now he's a potential B and E suspect.

No doubt our neighbourhood plight would qualify as pretty small *patates frites* to an Iraqi widow or a street kid in Tegucigalpa. What did we lose? A few dollars and a couple of yuppie gadgets.

But something else as well. We lost something you can't measure on a social worker's chart or pay for in your taxes. A sense of innocence? No, more like a presumption. The Real World paid us a wake-up call. We're still working on our response.

Jane Jacobs, the world-famous writer, philosopher and best friend North American neighbourhoods ever had, became a community activist after watching her favourite New York City neighbourhoods rot and fall apart. Her solution? She moved to Toronto where she's lived for more than thirty years. If Jane Jacobs thinks there's hope for Toronto, there's no reason for the rest of us to surrender our communities.

We just have to work a little harder at keeping them healthy.

CANADA: TOO SMALL FOR ITS OWN GOOD

I love my country—can we get that straight right from the get-go? I love it right down to its blackflies and cold snaps; yea, even unto Revenue Canada and Celine Dion. In terms of real estate, I wouldn't dream of moving anywhere else on the planet. In terms of citizenship, I will relinquish my Canuckhood only when they pry my Tim Horton coffee card from my cold, dead fingers.

However.

There is one thing about Canada that drives me absolutely nuts.

It's our smallness. Oh, I know we're huge geographically—biggest country in the world, now that Russia's been sliced and diced. But in many ways we can be smaller than a June bug's johnson—even toward ourselves. I'm talking about our relentless, tiresome self-deprecation. Was there ever a nation on earth more aw-shucks-humble than Canada? The blushing schoolboy routine might have been charming a hundred years ago when we actually were hewers of wood and drawers of water, but we're all grown up now. We have pubic hair and driver's licences and everything. It's about time we acted out age.

And Ralph Klein, if you're reading this, go out and brand a steer or something, because you don't want to hear what I'm going to say next.

It's about the results of a recent York University study on bilingualism. The study shows that speaking a second language actually *improves* the brain. Researchers tested the mental skills of bilingual speakers of Cantonese and English, Tamil and English, and French and English. The bilingualists consistently outperformed English-only speakers. Ellen Bialystok, a researcher at York University, explains that speaking a second language actually produces physical changes in the brain—it pumps more blood to carry more oxygen. "Being bilingual is like going to a brain gym," she says.

So do English-Canadians embrace the principle of official bilingualism, which amounts to a unique, government-sponsored opportunity to enrich our lives and broaden our horizons? Nah. We bitch and whine about "the Quebec conspiracy" and the immense burden of having to confront a few French words on our cornflakes boxes every morning.

Come on, Canada...stretch a little.

Then there's our smallness toward others, specifically our knee-jerk anti-Americanism. That's childish too—and kind of pathetic. Sure, Yanks can be obnoxious and bossy and stubborn and downright scary.

Just like Sheila Copps and Don Cherry.

And yes, they currently have a dangerous idiot for a president. But you know what? Come the next election, he's gone. It's a whole new ball game. And the next president will be elected by ballots, not bullets.

Which is not an option with the ayatollahs, imams, supreme chieftains, sultans, warlords, "dear leaders" and other assorted thugs who rule most of the rest of the world.

Before we cheap-shot the US, I think it behooves the average Canuck to ask himself a few questions. Where was the car you drive manufactured? How about the clothes on your back? How about the fact that you get to listen—and react to—voices as various as Rush Limbaugh and Michael Moore? And to eat fresh oranges and avocados in January?

As much as it galls doctrinaire leftoids, fate placed our homeland right next to the richest, most technologically advanced civilization in the history of this planet. That immutable fact has imbued Canadians with one of the highest standards of living in the world.

Is America perfect? Not even close. The US comes not just with warts, but with carbuncles, pustules, goiter, hives and great running sores.

Our neighbour may be sick and delusional, but she is our neighbour. And she is ailing, not terminal.

What if Canada—instead of sniping and griping and holier-than-thou-ing—worked at actually helping the folks next door?

That would be mighty big of us.

LET'S TAKE THE TURKS!

You know what this country needs? Not a five-cent cigar, a chicken in every pot or a Humvee in every carport. What this country needs is beachfront.

Oh, we've got plenty of *coastline*—more coastline than just about any other country in the world—but it ain't exactly Waikiki, is it? No Canuck in his right mind is going to saunter down to the shore in January to cop a few rays on a beach towel. Nope, Canada's definitely been shortchanged in the beachfront department. Our noisy cousins to the south have Florida and California, Australia has beaches coming out its kookaburra, Hawaii has...well, Hawaii. And Canada? Canada's got a few postage-stamp-sized swatches of sand that, unless you're a polar bear, are uninhabitable, basking-wise, for ten months out of twelve.

Let's face it: Canada needs to annex the Turks and Caicos Islands.

I'm talking about an idyllic necklace of tropical atolls nestled in the Caribbean just south of the Bahamas. Visualize, if you will, a half-dozen islands lightly dusted with about twenty-five thousand permanent residents who are forced to endure a relentless regimen of sunshine, golden beaches and an average yearly temperature of eighty degrees Fahrenheit.

And they're ripe for the plucking. In fact they're begging to be plucked. Politically they are a protectorate of Britain, but they're sick of being ignored by London and would love to join Canada. The Director of Tourism for the Turks and Caicos, John Skippings, isn't shy about it.

"Make us an offer," he said recently.

"We're going to be associated with somebody, and already, many of our businesses and resorts are Canadian-owned. There hasn't been much discussion about a union in recent years and we'd love to revisit it."

Mr. Skippings is referring to an historic shame that you won't find mentioned in Canadian history books—one that marks a pathetic pivotal point in the non-evolution of our country. I refer to that moment thirty years ago when Max Saltsman, a Member of Parliament from Ontario, put forth a private member's bill to annex the islands.

Think of it, Canada! An eleventh province composed primarily of palm trees, sand and surf. Where no one knows the meaning of terms like "snow shovel," "block heater" or "mittens."

Alas, Saltsman's visionary proposal died on the order paper. Those idiots in Ottawa, probably suffering from frostbitten frontal lobes, dismissed the idea out of hand.

We had another chance. In 1987 a delegation from the Turks and Caicos actually visited Ottawa, openly courting a deal. Our External Affairs Department did a study and advised against any such union. The report found "no benefit to Canadians in the union."

No benefit to Canadians? Have these bean-counters and pencil-pushers ever crossed Portage at Main in December? Have they tried to start a car on a Thunder Bay January morn? Stood at a bus stop in Prince George in February? Used a blowtorch to thaw the water pipes after a March blizzard in St. John's?

No benefits?

All right, I realize I'm becoming a little hysterical. That's because I have a personal interest. Back in 1987 I hosted a radio show on the CBC and word of the Turks and Caicos delegation to Ottawa reached me. I admit I mounted a modest campaign to assist the delegation. I interviewed them, made various approving noises, played a lot of Harry Belafonte and Bob Marley on my show and even offered to do a live broadcast from the islands to ah, focus international attention on their proposal. I even vowed to stay down there broadcasting live to Canada for as long as it took—even all winter.

And did CBC management do anything to bolster my campaign? Did they devote, oh, let's say even one ten-thousandth of the dough they routinely fork over to bankroll curling bonspiels and Stanley Cup semifinals?

They did not. No vision. Just like those dimwits in Ottawa.

But this time I've got backup. A group called Canadians for a Tropical Province is collecting signatures on a petition asking the feds to "officially study and rigorously pursue the notion of annexation" and to make the Turks-Caicos our eleventh province.

Well, sign me up, CFATP. Why should winter-weary Canucks continue to leave literally billions of loonies and toonies each year in the coffers of Honolulu, Myrtle Beach, San Miguel de Allende and other foreign destinations when we could be boosting the economy—and basting our backs—in our very own Caribbean province?

C'mon, Ottawa—flex a little. Try to think outside the igloo. And if takes an on-the-spot goodwill ambassador to make this happen, I'm your man.

I'm a little tied up right now, but November to April looks wide open.

PART II:
BANANAS IN THE WILD

CONFESSIONS OF A CARNIVORE

Went to a huge lobsterfest last week. Dozens of the bristly brutes had been express air-freighted in from PEI and boiled on the spot. Not surprisingly the place was packed with enthusiastic diners armed with forks and pincers, drooling onto their bibs. They weren't disappointed. Everybody got a hulking two or three-pounder hanging off both sides of the plate.

Except me. I settled for the potato salad, some sliced tomatoes and two buns.

It's not that I'm a vegetarian or even lobster-phobic; it's just that I prefer the food on my plate to be a little more gullet-ready. Any time you catch me with a pair of pliers in my hand and wearing a drop sheet, chances are I'm on my way to change the oil, not eat a meal.

On second thought, *do* put me down as lobster-phobic. I don't know what heinous crimes those creepy crustaceans committed in their previous karmic life but it must have been grim to look as evil as they do. Lobsters are indisputably ugly suckers, whether they're scuttling across the ocean floor or reclining on bone china. It's not your average life form that can manage to appear flamboyant and hideous at the same time. Lobsters look like steroid-pumped cockroaches in drag.

And there's the labour component. When you sit down to a lobster dinner, you don't just dig in; you have to deconstruct them first. You're not eating a meal—you're conducting an autopsy.

What really turns me off is that a lobster on the plate is so blatantly a creature lately deceased. Porterhouse steak is not like that. Neither are pork chops or chicken breasts. I'm more comfortable when the biological origins of my food are camouflaged. How many of us could cheerfully tuck into a lamb kabob if it arrived at our table looking remotely like the loveable, bleating, gambolling cutie it so recently was?

Hypocritical? You bet. Hypocrisy is the operative mode for your twenty-first century human carnivore. After all, very few of us kill, gut and dress our own meat these days, and a lot fewer of us would be carnivores if we did. I know, for once, whereof I speak. As a teenager I worked at the Ontario Public Stock Yards. I was an alley rat—a cane-waving middleman between the farmers who brought in their livestock and Canada Packers, the purchasers that, ah, "rendered" the beasts. I guarantee that if most Canadians spent one afternoon in a slaughterhouse, we would be known as a nation of lettuce eaters.

But we don't choose to put ourselves through that. Instead we buy our meat at the supermarket or the delicatessen, nicely sawn up, sculpted and vacuum-packed into amorphous portions like so many protein pucks. Oh, we won't eat absolutely *anything*. We wrinkle our noses at Europeans who eat horse and Indonesians who eat dog, but is that so very far removed from our taste for veal or squab? Aren't we just talking about different menus?

Me, I'm a most unlikely carnivore. I don't hunt. I don't fish. I even rescue spiders from the bathtub and relocate them on the woodpile by the side door. And yet I eat meat. How do I justify that? I don't. I just do it. I pretend that what's on my plate was not recently excised from a dewy-eyed Aberdeen Angus or a frolicking Dorset lamb. I just close my eyes, shut down my mind and chew.

Mind you, I would renounce my guilt-ridden habit and give up meat tomorrow, but for one thing.

It tastes so damn good.

I tried living without meat once. I was a vegetarian for two years. I inhaled more green than a Mastercraft lawnmower and sucked back more pasta than Pavarotti. But the gastronomic limitations got me in the end. I discovered that the lowly soybean curd is lowly for a reason.

And a man can eat only so many zucchini-goat cheese casseroles.

I respect and admire the old vegan adage about not eating "anything with a face." I just can't live up to it, that's all.

Just call me a reluctant carnivore. And a two-faced one, at that.

ANYONE HEARD FROM CHICKEN LITTLE?

Back in the bad old days of mining, when underpaid workers crawled and scrabbled through underground shafts with pick-axes and carbon-arc headlamps, the mine owners didn't spend a lot of time or money improving the air those miners were breathing. So the miners were forced to look out for themselves and they came up with an ingenious method of monitoring the underground air quality. They took down canaries in cages. Why canaries? Because the miners didn't have to watch them; they could hear them. Canaries sing pretty well all the time. When they're happy.

Canaries' songs change or stop completely when they're distressed or frightened. Or when the atmosphere around them turns threatening. Thus canaries could tell when trouble was in the air long before the miners would become aware of it.

There's a school of thought that says we could learn a lot more from animals, if only we could decode the messages they're sending us. What do we make, for instance, of the swarm of frogs that recently surrounded a home in Double Bay, Australia?

As near as anyone can figure, the frogs were drawn by the cries of a newborn child. Hours after baby Gwen Notley came home from the hospital, the frogs started showing up in the front yard. "By the end of the week, there were millions of frogs on our porch," says Gwen's father, Rourke. Scientists were flummoxed. Maybe the baby's cries sounded like a frog mating call? The Notleys finally moved to a frog-free suburb of Sydney.

Here in Canada we almost didn't have a Groundhog Day on February 2, 2003, due to an alarming shortage of groundhogs in Ontario. For years believers have crouched around a groundhog hole near Wiarton, Ontario, on February 2 to see whether or not Wiarton Willie would see his shadow—legend being that if he does, we're in for another six weeks of winter. (Or is it if he *doesn't* see his shadow? Doesn't matter. It's just a photo op for newspapers and an excuse to have a few beers.)

The point is that there has never—in all the years of Groundhog Day observing—been a problem with finding a groundhog. I grew up in a rural Ontario that had a lot of shortages—but never of groundhogs. Just about every farmer's field had a resident groundhog or two—sometimes whole colonies of them. And the rural roadsides were festooned with the remains of some of the slower ones. But in recent years, Ontario's groundhog population has nose-dived and no one is absolutely certain why.

Over in England, they're less worried about mineshaft canaries singing than the fact that they can't hear the chirp of a simple house sparrow. It wasn't long ago that the little grey and brown bird was considered a pest in British cities, towns and countrysides. Now it's almost disappeared. "The population has fallen by ninety-nine percent since 1980," says ornithologist Denise Summers-Smith. "This is almost extinction." So what's causing the virtual obliteration of a feisty little bundle of feathers that survived the Blitz, air pollution, British house cats *and* the music of Herman's Hermits?

Then there are the penguins at the San Francisco Zoo. Forty-six of them. They've been lazing around on the banks of their pond in the penguin enclosure for the past five years, preening their feathers and waiting for their three-squares-a-day zoo handouts.

Until the newcomers came.

Six new penguins were introduced to the enclosure last month. The newcomers instantly jumped in the pond and began swimming. Weirdly, the original forty-six jumped in also and began churning around the pond as fast as they could go.

And they're still doing it. The penguins swim until they collapse from exhaustion. They rest a while, then they get up and start the marathon again. "We've lost complete control," says a zoo official. "They've swum more in the last three weeks than they have in the past five years." The zookeepers even drained the pool in an effort to interrupt the behaviour. The penguins jumped in and marched around the bottom.

What's the deal? It's like the massing Australian frogs, the disappearing Ontario groundhogs and the brink-of-extinction British house sparrows—nobody knows for sure.

But it might be wrong to jump to apocalyptic conclusions. We mustn't forget the case of the Massachusetts two-headed toad.

This biological phenomenon was discovered by a four-year-old girl in Framingham, Massachusetts, and written up in the town's newspaper, the *Metro West Daily News*.

"The two amphibians are conjoined, unidentical twins," read the newspaper report.

A week later the paper printed a correction. What the girl had found was in fact two toads. Being extremely friendly with each other. "The male toad was hanging on for dear life," explained a local biologist.

Er. Precisely.

Freud was right. Sometimes a cigar is just a cigar.

DANGER! TEDDY BEARS AHEAD

Fear is essential. It is like a drug. Fear makes you think you will die. For that reason each moment has intensity. It is a kind of purification.

So spake a man who should know a thing or two about fear. Those are the words of Luis Miguel Dominguín, one of Spain's most famous bullfighters. Anyone who makes a living coaxing razor-sharp horns backed by eight hundred kilos of angry, galloping bull past his nether reaches is someone who simply has to know the meaning of fear. Some would call that brave; others would call it foolhardy. I call it a cop-out.

It's all very well for Dominguín to face down a fighting bull, but you'll notice that never once in his long career did he take on that most bloodthirsty and man-hating creature of the wild.

Yes, friends. I'm talking about the teddy bear.

Statistical fact: each year, more human beings are killed by teddy bears than by grizzly bears. How? Let me count the ways. Kids choke on those cute button eyes and loose tufts of fur. Besides—who knows where that teddy bear's been? Nursery school? In Fido's mouth? Viruses and bacteria can piggyback into your house on teddy's pelt and lay the whole family low with infections various and sundry.

I didn't discover the teddy bear's toxic secret—a writer by the name of Laura Lee did. She's just published a book entitled *100 Most*

Dangerous Things in Everyday Life and What You Can Do About Them.

What's really riveting about Lee's book is the revelation that, when it comes to life-threatening agents in your life, it's the little things you need to keep an eye on. It's the teddy bears, not the Iberian toros, that will do you in. Typically humans concentrate on the big picture and walk right into the open manhole. We go all white-knuckled at the prospect of boarding an airplane, but we're more likely to die in our own car driving down to Starbucks. We're paranoid about getting AIDS from a blood transfusion, but we're thirty times more likely to get struck by lighting than to be jabbed by a tainted hypodermic. Afraid of being mugged? You're far more likely to mug yourself by slipping on the bath mat in your own bathroom. And while you're in the bathroom—careful with the toothbrush, eh? Hospital emergency rooms treat more than twenty-five hundred people each year for injuries sustained while brushing their teeth. Always the little things.

What sort of little things? Oh, books. Doctor's neckties. Underwear.

Books are bad. ERs routinely handle more book casualties than many sports injuries. In Britain more people are hurt by books each year (2,707) than by training weights (1,884). And it's no better on this side of the pond. Karen Miller of the American Library Association says, "From working with books for many years, I could offer up things like broken toes when books fall, losing one's balance when reaching for books and repetitive stress from shelving them." And who hasn't ripped open a finger on a loose staple on a magazine spine? Or thrown out their back lugging a box of *National Geographic*s down to the basement?

We better hope that Al Qaeda keeps fixating on nuclear hardware and bioweapons. If the terrorists ever twig to the destructive potential of a Tom Clancy novel, we're cooked.

And neckties. Next time you're in for a medical checkup, be sure to ask for a doctor who's not wearing a necktie. Medicos see a lot of gross and grotty (not to mention infectious) stuff in a working day and sometimes they have to get up close and personal. You never know where that necktie dangled last. Nuff said.

And if you don't think underwear is a potential human threat then you haven't been keeping up with your UK Department of Trade and Industry bulletins. Last year the Department reported more than four hundred underwear-related mishaps ranging from two London women who were electrocuted when a bolt of lightning coursed through the metal wiring in one of their bras, to an unfortunate chap who sustained a fracture and ligament damage when his left middle finger became entangled in the bra strap of his overly enthusiastic paramour.

British Prime Minister Harold Macmillan once sagely observed that "to be alive at all involves some risk." How right he was—even if you don't mess with bras.

By the way, that bullfighter I mentioned? Luis Miguel Dominguín? Retired from the bullring after a thirty-six-year career. Died in his sleep in his seventies.

HAVE A BANANA

Time flies like an arrow.
Fruit flies like a banana.

Consider the humble banana. Was there ever a more perfect fruit? No leaves to shuck, no rinds to claw away, no pits or stones to loosen your fillings. No need to add sugar or milk or any other thing. Just unzip...and eat.

The banana is a delicious, convenient, self-contained meal. But even if it was as tart as rhubarb, as prickly as an artichoke and as impenetrable as a coconut, we would still be beholden to the banana. If only for its linguistic contributions.

We have banana seats on bicycles and banana peppers in the spice department. We have the banana fish, the banana boa and Harry Belafonte singing "The Banana Boat Song." Australia has the banana bird, Ontario has its banana belt, various Mafia families pay homage to their top bananas and second bananas...and South and Central America have all manner of tinpot dictatorships familiarly known as banana republics.

And where, pray tell, would humour be without the humble banana skin? Humour needs the banana skin. Stephen Leacock opined (although he disapproved) that the archetypal joke is the proverbial man walking down the street and slipping on the proverbial banana skin.

Whether the bard of Mariposa approved or not, there is something wonderfully amusing about the outsized, canary-hued, goofily phallic banana.

Too bad it's doomed.

Black Sigatoka is the culprit. It's a fungal disease that is lashing through banana plantations around the world even as I type. Don't they have fungicides that can knock out black Sigatoka? Well, yes, but that only helps for a while.

"As soon as you bring in a new fungicide," says one expert, "the fungi develop resistance. One thing we can be sure of is that the Sigatoka won't lose this battle."

The problem is intensified by the fact that the bananas we buy are highly hybridized. Bananas in the wild are scrawny, tough as leather and full of seeds—virtually inedible. Over the centuries growers cultivated various mutant strains that had a sweet taste and no seeds. No seeds in the banana is a real plus for the eater, but it means the fruit is sterile; it can't be crossed with other strains to breed for disease resistance.

So is the situation hopeless? Some experts think so. A recent edition of the *New Scientist* contains an article saying flatly that the banana as we know it could be a thing of the past within ten years.

There's always the potential of new and more powerful fungicides, but that's not a mouth-watering prospect. Neither is another possibility: the genetically modified banana. Researchers have already developed genetically modified bananas that are resistant to black Sigatoka, but lots of folks—including a writer I know—are very leery of popping genetically tinkered comestibles down their cake holes.

But this is solemn stuff. Far too sober-sided for a treat as inherently cheerful as your humble banana. Let me leave you with the only banana joke I know.

It's a story about a bus conductor. He works a downtown bus in Dallas. One day he rings the bell just as a passenger is coming through the door. The driver takes off and the passenger is run over and killed. This being Texas, the conductor is put on trial, found guilty and sentenced to the electric chair. Comes the day of his execution, and he's about to be strapped in the chair. The executioner asks if he has any last requests.

"Well," says the guy, "is that your lunch over there?" The executioner tells him it is. "Could I have your banana?"

The executioner gives the condemned man his banana, allows him to eat it, then straps him down and throws the switch. When the smoke clears, the guy is sitting in the chair looking around, totally unharmed. The executioner can't believe it.

"Can I go now?" asks the guy.

"I suppose so," says the executioner. "This has never happened before."

The conductor is released, gets back his old job on the bus and six months later the same thing happens. He rings his bell before the riders have boarded, the bus takes off and another rider is run over. The conductor gets the death penalty again, and exactly the same scenario unfolds. He eats the executioner's banana, the switch is thrown, millions of volts course through his body—the room fills with smoke and when it clears the guy is sitting in the chair unharmed.

"This is insane!" yells the executioner. "What's your secret? Is it the bananas?"

"Not really," says the guy in the chair. "I'm just a really bad conductor."

NOTHING STUNS LIKE A DEER

Here's a little quiz for you to while away the time waiting for the barkeep to refill the pretzel bowl—what do you reckon is the most dangerous animal in North America?

Well, the Yanks are way ahead of us on this one. They've got scorpions, diamondback rattlers, coral snakes and black widow spiders, not to mention gators, great white sharks and Bill O'Reilly. But Canada can post some pretty impressive predators. Your Rocky Mountain grizzly—there's a fella you don't want to pester for spare change. Cougars pack some pretty impressive switchblade cuticles, not to mention their dental armoury. We've got our very own viper—the Eastern Massasauga Rattlesnake—not to mention Wood Buffalo bison, wolverines, timber wolves, muskoxen, wharf rats, rabid bats. Heck, even the lowly mosquito can punch your ticket if it happens to be packing West Nile virus in its stinger.

But none of these can hold a candle nor a canine tooth to the most dangerous critter on the continent.

It's Rudolph.

Which is to say your common, timid, vegetarian, non-belligerent white-tail deer. This year Bambi and his brethren will knock off more North American primates than all predatory forms of wildlife combined.

And how do they do it? The hard way, mostly—by stepping out in front of our cars and trucks at inopportune moments. Needless to say, this manoeuvre hurts them a lot more than it does us. In the US, deer-vehicle collisions constitute more than a million traffic incidents every year. Mostly the deer involved pay with their lives. Even so, more than twenty-nine thousand Americans can expect to be injured in such a crash in any given year, more than two hundred of them fatally.

The numbers here in Canada are lower but no less alarming. Even Saskatchewan, which boasts the most wide open of spaces, racks up 3,620 deer-vehicle collisions annually.

And we've got no one to blame but ourselves. Since the day the white man arrived, we've systematically wiped out the wolf, cougar and bear populations in most parts of the continent. This has left the deer bereft of natural predators. Which means the deer population has exploded to...well, to levels they probably enjoyed before the pale guys in the big sailboats first landed.

Except that it isn't the same "here" anymore. We've gobbled up hundreds of thousands of square miles of natural deer habitat with our logging, our subdivisions and our road networks. Which means more and more deer on less and less land.

And that means trouble. In many parts of North America the vast numbers of deer are stripping the forests of vegetation. Gary Alt, a wildlife biologist with the Pennsylvania Game Commission, fears that eventually "everything will be lost. The deer population will not be healthy and scores of other species will suffer."

Interestingly enough, the situation is reversed on Vancouver Island. There, deer herds are said to be in decline. One of the provincial governments more brilliant proposed solutions? Kill off a slew of wolves and mountain lions to "take the pressure off the deer."

And incidentally leave more deer for human hunters to make sport with.

There's another island that could teach us all an important lesson in wildlife management. It's called Isle Royale. You'll find it tucked into the northwest corner of Lake Superior. Isle Royale is uninhabited by humans, but has a goodly population of wolves, moose and deer. Logging, hunting and development have been banned on Isle Royale for most of the last century and all of this one. The animals have been pretty much left to themselves.

So did the deer and moose strip the island bare? Did the wolves proliferate and eat the deer and moose right down to the last rib-eye steak?

Nope, the populations stabilized themselves naturally, without benefit of biologists, government planners or gun-toting "harvesters."

We tend to forget that Mother Nature somehow muddled through for thousands of years before we came along to help her. Which means we really should rethink that notion about the whitetail deer as public enemy number one. The most dangerous animal in North America isn't the ungulate in the headlights.

It's the monkey behind the wheel.

FEELING NO PAIN

I don't recall all the comic books I devoured in my misspent youth, but I do remember one of them. It was called *Haunted Tales* and it specialized in creepy stories calculated to send shivers of dread down impressionable prepubescent spines.

I even remember one particular story in *Haunted Tales*. The first panel showed a close-up of a delicious looking chocolate bar, still in its shiny wrapper, lying on a dock by a lake. Along comes a middle-aged looking guy with a fishing rod over his shoulder, obviously out for a day of angling. He spies the chocolate bar, picks it up, unwraps it and pops it in his mouth with a contented smile.

In the next panel he's dropped the fishing rod and his eyes are as big as golf balls. His mouth is all puckered and distended—and now you can see a thin, taut line running from the corner of his mouth straight across the dock and into the water. The fisherman is on his knees and he's being dragged—reeled in—inexorably across the dock. The last panel of the story is a close-up of the lake surface with just a few bubbles rising and the fisherman's hat floating beside them.

The story was a rather clever, if unlikely, morality play designed to make the reader think about angling from a different…angle, as it were. The moral being, "What if fish did to us what we do to them?"

Except...not.

Anybody who's ever hooked a fish—be it a sixty-pound tyee or a six-inch chub—knows that what you get right from the get-go is A Fight. The fish struggles, resists, tries with every muscle in its body to shake that hook out of its jaw.

Now imagine yourself in place of that fish on the line, with a great big treble hook set deep in your cheek. (And imagine that, like a fish, you have no arms to grab the line and relieve the pressure.) Would you be shaking your head and bucking your weight against the hook? No. You would be whimpering and mincing and tippy-toeing ever so rapidly in whatever direction the hook was pulling you. That's because we human beings have oodles of nerve endings in our cheeks. A hook in the cheek would hurt plenty.

Whereas fish—at least in the bony cartilage of their mouths—have no such nerve endings. That's why they can put up a fight when they're hooked.

Now I know I'm going to get letters on this—especially from the PETA folks. PETA—that's People for the Ethical Treatment of Animals—has already spent millions of dollars on a campaign to outlaw angling, which it considers barbaric.

All I can say is, save yourself a stamp.

Get in touch instead with James D. Rose at the University of Wyoming. As a professor of zoology and physiology, he's been working on the ins and outs of fish neurology for the past three decades. Recently Professor Rose published a study that compares the nervous systems of fish and mammals. His conclusion? Fish lack the brainpower to sense pain or fear.

But a minnow sees a largemouth bass coming at him and flees—isn't that fear? No, says Professor Rose, that's nociception—responding to a threatening stimulus. Which he contends is an entirely different kettle of...well, you know. According to Professor Rose's report, the awareness of pain depends on functions of specific regions of the cerebral cortex that fish simply do not possess.

So it looks like PETA's out of luck with their anti-angling crusade—but wait a minute! What about bait? Doesn't live bait suffer from cruel and unusual punishment?

Not necessarily. I remember the time I was ice fishing on a lake north of Thunder Bay. It was bitterly cold, and I wasn't getting a nibble.

Just then an old Finlander settles in about thirty yards away, bores a hole in the ice, drops in a line and starts hauling in fish after fish. Finally I can't stand it. I walk over to him and say, "Excuse me, but I've been here all day and I haven't had a bite. You've been here half an hour and you've got a dozen on your string. What's your secret?"

"Roo raff roo reep ra rurms rarm," he says.

I say, "Sorry, I didn't catch that."

"Roo raff roo reep ra rurms rarm."

I say, "Sounds like you're speaking Finnish—can you tell me in English?"

With a look of disgust he spits a slimy brown ball into his mitten and says, "You have to keep the worms warm!"

REFUGEES WELCOME, PIT BULLS NEED NOT APPLY

Salt Spring Island has an interesting history as a kind of United Nations sanctuary. West Coast First Nations people regarded it as a healing place and used it as such, probably for thousands of years. Much later it became a refuge for disgruntled Sandwich Islanders—Hawaiians to us, Kanakas to themselves. They came to Salt Spring, liked what they saw, and stayed. Ex-slaves from the American south came to Salt Spring in the late nineteenth century, and some of their descendants still live here. Not so long ago a significant number of Americans opposed to the Vietnam War took up residence on Salt Spring. We're seeing another population bulge right now made up of American ex-pats who don't share George Dubya's evangelical world vision. And an even more recent entry in Salt Spring's haven ledger. The island has just become the last stop in an underground railway...for pit bulls.

Yep, I sing of Moxie, an eight-week-old pit bull puppy that was recently flown in from Windsor, just ahead of a proposed Ontario ban on the breeding of his kind. Predictably this no-more-pit-bulls proposal by the Ontario government spawned a media frenzy, with headlines blaring of "death row puppies" and "doomed pit bulls whisked to safety."

Pit bull champion Cathy Prothro denounced Ontario's ban as "racial profiling" and "ethnic cleansing."

The facts were somewhat less hysterical. True, Ontario brought in pit bull legislation. But it did not involve the dispatch of squads of SWAT teams à la King Herod to smite the first-born in every kennel. It's the *breeding* of pit bulls they wanted stopped. Pit bulls which were already alive in Ontario were to be spayed or neutered and required to wear a muzzle in public places. Any Ontario pit bulls that died did so because their owners couldn't be bothered abiding by the new legislation.

Defenders of the breed point out that not all dog attacks are by pit bulls. That's true. Dobermans bite. German shepherds bite. Hell, Shih Tzus and Pomeranians and chihuahuas can bite you. The difference between getting bitten by a pit bull and, say, a cocker spaniel is the difference between getting bitten by a great white shark and a brook trout.

Pit bulls don't all bite, but when they do, they bite for keeps. They have incredibly powerful, bone-crushing jaws and they don't let go. I once interviewed a Toronto police officer and asked him what I should do if I was attacked by a pit bull. He replied, "Offer it your least useful arm."

I couldn't find records for Canada, but in the US, pit bulls are responsible for more than twice as many fatal attacks as the next most dangerous breed. Them's the facts, folks.

Some people argue that it's the owners of pit bulls who should be punished when their dogs run amok, but that's scant comfort to the parents of a child who's had her face ripped off while playing in a park.

Personally I could get behind a movement to spay all *owners* of pit bulls to put a crimp in their breeding program, but that's not gonna fly. So I'd settle for legislation that requires pit bulls to be leashed and muzzled when in public.

And that, I'm afraid, goes for Moxie on Salt Spring, adorable as the pit bull puppy undoubtedly is. I'm sure Moxie will pick up on the laid-back Salt Spring ambience and spend the rest of his life as benign as Benji, sniffing daffodils and peeing on fence posts and biting no one.

But wouldn't it be awful if I was wrong?

GIVING GEESE THE BIRD

If we could have a minute of silence I'd declare it right now. In honour of Bob Gillespie. Mr. Gillespie, a town councillor in Saanich, British Columbia, recently had the temerity to suggest that we should start shooting Canada geese that are infesting and befouling his town's water reservoir. He went further than that. He suggested somebody should open a new café specializing in gooseburgers.

Bob, Bob, Bob...what were you thinking? That's blasphemy, Bob. If not treason. Why not just burn down Anne of Green Gables's house? Why not keelhaul a beaver?

You can't shoot Canada geese sitting on a reservoir, Bob. They're warm and they're fuzzy. Why, they're almost as cute as those harp seals on the East Coast that Brigitte Bardot's so worked up about. You don't want Brigitte Bardot on your case, Bob.

But cheer up—it could be worse. You could be Sir Peter Maxwell Davies.

Sir Peter, who lives on the Orkney Islands off the north coast of Scotland, is a very big deal in British musical circles. As a matter of fact his official title is Queen's Composer. He is also an eminently practical man, so when a whooper swan (about the same size and heft as one of our BC trumpeter swans) flew into a power line near Sir Peter's home and flash-barbecued itself, he decided to make the best of a grisly situation. He picked up the carcass and took it home. Being a conscientious environmentalist, he also phoned the Royal Society for the Protection of Birds to inform it of the creature's unfortunate demise. The society thanked him and advised him to "dispose of" the dead bird.

You bet, thought Sir Peter, with visions of whipping up a mouth-watering swan terrine. Sir Peter must have done his culinary musing out loud, because a covey of cherry-flashing police cars materialized soon after in his front yard. They impounded the defunct fowl and warned Sir Peter that he had been flirting with a prison sentence for interfering with a protected species.

Had Sir Peter fed the carcass to his cat or thrown it over a fence, there would have been no problem. The fact that he planned to cook it up and eat it himself shifted him to the "criminal intent" category.

A cautionary tale that reflects the wacky times we live in. As does the story of Councillor Gillespie, who is no doubt fielding his share of calls from constituents outraged that he wants to knock off a few geese just because they're contaminating his town's water supply. Bambi syndrome they call it.

Perhaps they both could take some comfort from the story that appeared on the front page of *Burnaby Now* a few years ago.

It detailed attempts to control the proliferation of flamingeese, weird mutant birds that resulted from the mating of a flamingo and a Canada goose and were threatening to take over Burnaby Lake. The newspaper story, based on interviews with international wildlife experts Enrico Palri and Brad Lofos, told of plans to destroy all the eggs in flamingoose nests around the periphery of the lake. Readers were outraged. Environmentalists fumed and little old ladies fretted. A website to save the Canadian flamingoose was even launched.

Reaction was so swift and fierce that scarcely any readers noticed that the last names of the experts—Palri and Folos—could be rearranged to spell Fools…and April.

The story appeared in the pages of *Burnaby Now* in 1989. On April 1 to be exact.

There's your out, councillor. Just issue a news release explaining that it was an early April Fool's joke.

DON'T DRINK THE H_2O!

How's this for a delightful, ground-breaking idea? The prime minister has announced the formation of an Anti-Absurdity Bureau to deal with the government's excessive foolishness.

That's the good news. The bad news is the prime minister's name is Einars Repše, not Paul Martin. And the country he presides over is Latvia, not Canada.

Oh, well. It's a start.

Lord knows the Great White North could use an Anti-Absurdist Ministry—if only to tackle the ongoing farce of airport security.

I approach the airport security desk en route from Victoria to Toronto. As I pass through the body scanner, my car keys, my wallet and my toiletries bag are rolling down the belt toward the x-ray machine.

"Whoa! What's this?" growls the rent-a-cop squatted on a stool by the x-ray monitor.

What's he unearthed? A switchblade? A grenade launcher? A half-pound of plastique moulded into the shape of a Winnie the Pooh toothpaste dispenser?

No. He has uncovered a tiny mechanical device with rotary blades and a cunning design that allows it to be concealed within the palm of oh, say, a wacko extremist suicide Al Qaeda terrorist bent on taking over an Air Canada flight and wreaking havoc in the air, somewhere between Horsefly, BC, and Punkeydoodles Corners, Ontario.

He has uncovered my nose-hair clippers.

"You can't take this on board," he declaims.

"It's a pair of clippers," I murmur with some embarrassment. "For...you know...nose hairs."

You actually want to grab the dork by the earlobes and say, "Look, moron! Can you imagine *anybody* trying to commandeer a 747 brandishing a dollar ninety-eight's worth of made-in-Hong-Kong imitation-stainless-steel facial foliage trimmer?" But you don't, because you know it will bring out the Mounties and a drug-sniffing German shepherd and several hours of imbecilic questions in a tiny, poorly ventilated room.

So you sigh and shrug and surrender your nose-hair clippers.

Could be worse. You could be a Nelson. More specifically a David Nelson.

You *really* don't want to be flying through the US with a passport bearing the name David Nelson these days. You'll *never* get through security without an extreme hassle.

Anytime anyone named David Nelson checks in for a flight anywhere in the US, the bells go off and the cops come out. Recently it happened to six David Nelsons in the Los Angeles area, eighteen in Oregon and four in Alaska. Why? Nobody seems to know—or at least wants to explain. The US Transportation Security Administration insists that the name David Nelson is not on any "terrorist list." They say perhaps the "name-matching technology" currently employed at airport checkpoints matches "the presence of letters in a name."

Whatever the hell that means.

What it means to me is that if my name was David Nelson, I'd be thinking about a vacation close to home this year.

The supreme irony of the terrorism scare is that, for all of the western world's technological sophistication, it's amazing how vulnerable we are. Vulnerable and gullible to the most outrageous attacks of boneheaded bureaucratic overkill.

Last spring a student at Eagle Rock Junior High won first prize in the Greater Idaho Falls Science Fair. His entry? A petition to the people demanding immediate government action on a dangerous chemical compound currently swirling through the land.

This was no joke. The odourless, tasteless liquid in question—dihydrogen monoxide—presents a clear and present danger to the public at large. Without proper supervision, it can cause excessive sweating and vomiting—not to mention severe burns in its gaseous state. Thousands of people have died from it through accidental inhalation.

It is also a major component of acid rain, erosion, and the physical degradation of metals. Doctors don't talk about it publicly but they know that most tumours of terminal cancer patients are riddled with pockets of dihydrogen monoxide.

The petition asked people if they supported a ban of this dangerous chemical compound. Hell, yes! Out of fifty respondents, forty-three said they wanted the government to act now to declare dihydrogen monoxide a dangerous and illegal substance. Six of the people petitioned were undecided and wanted more time to think about it.

Only one said, "Dihydrogen monoxide. Wait a minute. Isn't that another name for…water?"

NESSIE: MISSING AND PRESUMED DEAD

BULLETIN! BULLETIN! It's confirmed: the Loch Ness monster is missing. The alert comes from the Official Loch Ness Monster Fan Club, headquartered in Inverness, Scotland. The president of the club, Gary Campbell, reports, "There has been an unusually low number of sightings reported this year, all of which were made by local people. It appears that no tourists visiting the area have seen anything strange whilst at the loch."

Unusual indeed. People have been routinely and regularly reporting odd splashings and swirlings of outsized, scaly undulating critters from the banks of Loch Ness since 565 AD. That's when St. Columba reputedly stared down a serpent-like behemoth and sent it scuttling back into the tea-brown depths of Great Britain's largest body of fresh water.

Deep water too. If a giant marine monster was going to pick any lake in the land to hide in, Loch Ness would be number one on the list. It's almost a thousand feet deep in places, and experts suspect there may be a few rifts and canyons that go even deeper than that.

If there was a Nessie, it would have to be one elusive creature. People have been peering and poking and prodding the lake waters for the past fifteen hundred years, and no one has yet come up with any conclusive proof of the beast's existence. Oh, sure, there have been a few amateur photographs and some grainy video footage, but nothing that couldn't be explained away as playful otters, twists of driftwood, currents, wind or a trick of the light.

Not that they haven't tried to nail Nessie down. Over the years investigators have trawled the loch with underwater cameras, sonar transceivers, closed-circuit TV cameras—they've even used minisubmarines.

Nothing.

In the summer of 2003, the British Broadcasting Corporation decided to answer the question once and for all. They dispatched a team of researchers to conduct the most exhaustive search ever. They used satellite navigation technology and six hundred separate sonar beams to pore over ever cubic foot of the loch. "We went from shoreline to shoreline, top to bottom, on this one," said Ian Florence, one of surveyors. "We have covered everything in this loch and we saw no sign of any large living animal in the loch."

The BBC conclusion? The Loch Ness monster is a Loch Ness myth. That means the end of Nessie.

Not.

Nessie is a star, known around the world. Type "Loch Ness monster" into an internet search engine and you will come up with nearly half a million sites. Nessie won't die. Too many people need her.

We need our orcs and our trolls, our vampires and ghouls, our werewolves and ogres and zombies. So what if nobody's ever conclusively documented the existence of Ogopogo in Lake Okanagan or Cadborosaurus off Victoria?

We live in a world where sentient human beings believe in their paranoia-racked hearts that JFK was murdered by the CIA, the moon landing was staged in the Arizona desert and Princess Diana was snuffed by the British secret service.

A recent poll shows that an astounding twenty percent of the German population believes the US government ordered the September 11 attacks *on itself.* In an effort to restore sanity, the respected German newspaper *Der Spiegel* recently published a sixteen-page point-by-point refutation of myths and half-truths held as gospel by conspiracy theorists.

Will it change any minds? Of course not. As American political scientist Michael Barkun writes, "The wonderful thing about a conspiracy theory is that it allows you to understand everything perfectly. It discloses to you that all the evil in the world can be attributed to a single cause, and that 'they' are this cause, whoever 'they' might be."

Which brings us to the true fate of Nessie. She's not dead. She's confined in a holding tank at Guantanamo Bay in Cuba under suspicion of global terrorism.

I know it for a fact. Elvis told me.

FRIENDS, ROMANS, COUNTRYSKFXRLCH

Writing is simple: you just jot down amusing ideas as they occur to you. The jotting presents no problem; it's the occurring that is difficult.
—Stephen Leacock

One thing that just about everybody who doesn't do it for a living knows for sure: being a writer doesn't qualify as a real job. Writers get used to the old one-two punch at cocktail parties and barbecues. A stranger asks you what you do; you tell them you're a writer. And they come back with, "No, I meant what do you do for a *living*."

And even if they believe you, they still think it's kind of frivolous. An eminent Canadian brain surgeon once made the mistake of telling Margaret Laurence over the hors d'oeuvres that when he retired he planned to become a writer.

"What a coincidence," responded Laurence sweetly. "When I retire, I plan to take up brain surgery."

I don't know how the profession of writing got the dubious rap, but I suspect it might be laid at the doorstep of Thomas Huxley, a nineteenth-century British scientist and big supporter of Charles Darwin's theory of evolution. Huxley is the bloke who posited the popular notion that if an infinite number of monkeys sat down in front of an infinite number of typewriters and hunted and pecked for an infinite number of years, they would eventually type out the complete works of Shakespeare.

Whether or not his contention is true, the subtext is pretty clear:

writing is no big deal. Given enough time, even a chimp could be a great writer.

Not surprisingly a lot of writers demurred, but the idea caught on anyway and over the years began to take on the patina of accepted truth. It even extended to other potential bards in the animal kingdom. Recently Nathan Banks, an artist in New York, painted randomly chosen words on about sixty meandering members of a Holstein herd, in order to see if they would eventually line up and form something approaching a Petrarchan sonnet.

Meanwhile in England a writer by the name of Valerie Laws attempted to, as she put it, "break down the barriers between literature and quantum mechanics" by painting the words of one poem on the flanks of a flock of sheep, hoping that the sheep would rearrange themselves to form a brand new poem.

John Milton, eat your heart out.

Still, we shouldn't be too quick to scoff at the abilities of our fellow creatures. I remember only too well what happened when my bearded collie, Homer, decided to apply for a part-time job at a large metropolitan daily.

Making his rounds one morning, he'd seen an ad in the window of the newspaper office that read, "Help wanted. Must be bilingual and be able to type and handle a computer. We are an equal opportunity employer."

Homer went in, trotted up to the receptionist and barked. When she looked down, he walked over, sat in front of the sign and whined. She got the idea and took the dog in to see the editor. "I think he wants the job," she said, and they both laughed.

While they're laughing, Homer hops over to a vacant typewriter, rolls in a piece of paper and starts typing out his resumé. He finishes the page, signs it with a paw print, takes it to the editor in his mouth and then sits perfectly, his tail thumping expectantly.

"I-I-I can't hire you—you're a dog!" says the editor. "Besides, the ad says you have to be able to use a computer."

Homer leaps up, stands on his hind legs so he can reach the keyboard and fires up a nearby Macintosh iBook. He runs off two spreadsheets, reprints the help wanted ad in bold face and italic and proofreads a short accident report, finding two spelling mistakes and one dangling participle.

The editor is dumbfounded. "Look, you are very intelligent and obviously have more than enough technical skills, but I still can't hire you because, because...*dammit, you're a dog*!"

With just a hint of reproach, Homer pulls the sign out of the window, puts it on the editor's lap and lays a paw on the part about being an equal opportunity employer.

"Well I *still* can't hire you! The ad says you have to be bilingual!"

Homer looks him in the eye, opens his mouth and says, "Meow."

PART III:

OF MICE AND MACHINES

THE PHONE-Y WAR

In the beginning, long distance conversations pretty much depended on how loud you could shout. Leather-lunged chatters could comfortably make themselves heard from cave-mouth to cave-mouth. Then we developed smoke signals. Conversations—necessarily brutish and short—could be carried out from mountaintop to mountaintop, providing you had enough fuel, a sturdy blanket, no wind and a reliable flint.

Then on March 10, 1876, Alex Bell, bless his Edinburghian-Cape Bretonian-Bostonian heart, strung some electrified wire between two rooms and shouted, "Mr. Watson, come here, I need you," into one end of the wire. And Mr. Watson, hearing Bell's voice through the wire, came on the run.

That's the official story, anyway. My guess is, Bell yelled loud enough to be heard right through the wall, but no matter, the principle was sound. History says the world's first telephone call had been placed and answered.

It's been downhill ever since.

The Bell contraption begat the cumbersome wall telephone which begat the clunky handheld dial telephone, which began the hernia-inducing military walkie-talkie, the CB radio and eventually the light-as-a-feather, cute-as-a-bug's-ear plastic gizmo that you see in just about every second person's hand these days—usually jammed up against their earhole as they drive or walk or shop or sit on a park bench or eat their lunch—the cellphone.

And cellphone use is multiplying like a galloping rogue virus. Between 2000 and 2004, cellphone ownership in Canada grew by fifty-five percent. Nearly fourteen million Canadians are currently wireless subscribers. Experts say that by this time next year, fully fifty percent of us will be "wired for yakking."

Is that a bad thing? Not for the travelling salesman, the shut-in, the housewife whose car has broken down on the side of the Trans-Canada, or the hiker who's fractured a femur on the Juan de Fuca Marine Trail, but for...oh, say, eighty-five percent of the schnooks who buy, lug and natter into their cellphones every day, what's the point?

I had a cellphone once. I used it primarily to tell my partner each workday evening that I was off the train and in my car and headed home for dinner.

She knew that already. It was my regular pattern, with or without the call. Most of the calls I (am forced to) overhear each day are equally fatuous and a stone waste of everybody's time.

Which would rate as one of modern life's minor annoyances—along with traffic jams, email spam and the vocal stylings of Celine Dion—if that were the extent of the cellphone's depredations. It's not. The fact is, the popularity of the cellphone represents the death knell for a true communications breakthrough.

The phone booth.

The public phone booth has been around for more than a century. It has provided shelter from the storm, surcease from traffic noise, a cone of silence for personal conversations and a handy place for cross-dressing Clark Kent to assume his superhero alter ego.

All that's changing now. Canada lost nearly twenty thousand pay phones in the four years between 1999 and 2003. In Chicago, where the first one was installed in 1898, the public phone booth no longer exists at all.

And in Britain, home of world-famous fire-engine red telephone booth, the news is even grimmer. Authorities are cold-bloodedly plotting the extinction of the British icon. There are still fifteen thousand of them scattered across the flanks of Albion. BT Payphones plans to eliminate ten thousand public phone booths by this time next year.

The reasoning is bottom line, as usual. Four out of five Brits now carry cellphones. Phone booth revenue is down. Ergo, axe the phone booths.

Before they send the last phone booth to the knacker's yard, they might want to schedule a business lunch at the Brooklyn Café in Atlanta, Georgia. Or at the Main Street Bistro in Sarasota, Florida. Or at the trendy Spoke Club in Toronto.

The management in all three institutions is planning to install vintage red British telephone booths in their lobbies so that restaurant patrons can carry on conversations in private...on their cellphones.

Oh, right...private phone calls. Didn't we have those once?

IT'S ALL THE RAGE

I have a dead mouse nailed to my office wall. I killed it personally. With my bare hands.

Don't call the SPCA—this is not the four-legged, furry, cheese-lusting kind of mouse. My wall trophy is plastic. It's the gizmo that you palpate to move around the little arrow on your computer monitor. I've never been abidingly fond of my computer, but one day when it did something profoundly annoying, I was, as they say, somewhat overcome with emotion. I felt an intense desire to wrench the device from my desk and pitch it overhand through the window, but that would have been expensive. It would also have let the flies in. That's when my eye fell upon my wee mouse, quivering on its mouse pad. I balled my right fist and brought it down like the hammer of Thor.

Set me back $19.95, but my, it felt grand.

I'm not the first person to go postal over a computer. As a matter of fact, a recent study revealed that fifty percent of web surfers lose their tempers at least once a week.

It's not just computers, of course—we're living in the Age of Rage. Testosterone-heavy drivers who used to glare at each other and perhaps tap their horn once or twice now exchange obscene gestures, foam at the mouth and cut each other off. Road Rage.

And of course there's Air Rage. A British banker by the name of Finneran flipped out on a flight from Buenos Aires to New York last year, assaulting three flight attendants and defecating on a food trolley.

A simple "I'm not hungry" would have been sufficient, sir.

But when I heard about the assault on the woman dressed as an Italian sausage, I knew that Rage Rage was getting out of hand. Happened during a baseball game in Milwaukee last month. A woman dressed as an Italian sausage, accompanied by a colleague wearing a hot dog costume (I am not making this up), was running around the bases between innings as part of a fast food ad campaign. One of the ball players teasingly tapped the Italian sausage impersonator with his bat, the sausage lost its balance and knocked over the human hot dog and—Hey, presto!—an incident. The ball player was (I'm not making this up either) led off the diamond in handcuffs by gun-toting cops. An advertising executive speaking for the jostled meat puppets—perhaps overreacting ever so slightly—intoned, "This is one of the most outrageous things I've ever seen inside a ballpark or outside a ballpark. It sickened me to see it."

Yeah. Mascot Rage. Life doesn't get any uglier than that.

Or maybe it does. Come with me now to a quiet, leafy *cul de sac* in the city of Lincoln, England. You see that yellow line of police tape encircling that modest cottage? Murder investigation. The cottage owner got shot to death last week. By his next-door neighbour.

Because his hedge was too high.

That's right, Hedge Rage, and it's not the first fatal case. Last May a seventy-four-year-old homeowner in Louth, Lincolnshire, died of a heart attack following a fistfight with his neighbour over a hedge dispute.

I should point out that we're not talking little mulberry bushes here. The hedges that are causing all the trouble are Leyland cypresses, monster trees that shoot up like bamboo on steroids. They easily grow to thirty feet and they're very popular with Brits.

Well, with some Brits. For those who hate 'em there's Hedgeline. It's a support group with its very own website and it lobbies on behalf of people with grievances. About hedges. A spokesman for Hedgeline estimates there are more than a hundred thousand victims living involuntarily in the shade of their neighbour's hedges throughout the UK.

Well, fine...but a *website*?

That's all I'd need. My neighbour throws up a giant wall of cypresses that plunges my home into perpetual darkness. Do I protest or sneak out with a chainsaw during a thunderstorm? No. I'm a good, polite Canuck. I turn on my computer and tap in www.hedgeline.uk.

And an hourglass appears. And I wait. And wait. And wait. And finally, as cobwebs begin to enshroud my keyboard, my screen tells me, "This page cannot be displayed."

Followed by, "This program has performed an illegal operation and will be shut down."

Followed by a pop-up ad for Microsoft Windows Megapixel System 9.5.

To hell with it. Kill your mouse. It's more satisfying.

CYCLE PSYCHOLOGY

The bicycle has done more to emancipate women than anything else in the world.
—Susan B. Anthony

A woman needs a man like a fish needs a bicycle.
—Irina Dunn

It's been a long and somewhat bumpy ride for the familiar two-wheeler. Baron von Drais started it all. Away back in 1817 the eccentric German hammered together a contraption that became known as the Draisienne. It was made of wood, with wheels, a seat and handle-bars but no pedals. In order to ride the Draisienne, you had to shuffle your feet along the ground. The Draisienne did not go platinum.

A couple of decades later a Scotsman by the name of Macmillan improved on von Drais's hobby horse. He added swinging cranks on the front wheel which were connected to rods and levers to the back wheel. The whole thing was made of iron and weighed about sixty pounds. It too was something less than a bestseller.

In 1870 the first real bicycle, the penny farthing, was invented. It got its name from the difference in size between the wheels—the front wheel looked like a big English penny, the back wheel like a tiny farthing. It took a lot of skill to stay upright on the penny farthing and even if you did the ride was bone-crushing, thanks to the solid tires.

By the time I came along, which is to say firmly nestled in the glut of post-World-War-II baby boomers, the bicycle makers pretty much had it right. Their new improved product was light, the tires were filled with air, the seats were soft and the pedalling, thanks to a chain drive, was easy.

I still remember my very first bike. It was a blue-and-white CCM one-speed with a leather seat and a push bell screwed to the handlebars. Why, I cut my teeth (my shins and knuckles, actually) on that piece of technological wizardry.

State of the art. Yep, by the middle of the twentieth century, bicycles had gone about as far as they could go.

We thought.

No one was aware of it, but the winds of change were already licking at the kickstands of the bicycle world as we knew it. One day Tommy Farmer rode into the schoolground pedalling what might as well have been a UFO. It was a racing bike with drop handlebars and brakes mounted on the handlebars right next to a little gizmo none of us had seen before.

It was a chrome-plated Sturmey-Archer gearshift with a tiny lever you could move with your thumb. Imagine! A bicycle with three speeds—first, second and third! Suddenly the rest of us felt like we were riding Draisiennes.

But of course it was only the beginning. Europeans invented derailleurs which led to the creation of five-speed bikes and then ten-speed bikes. The concept of getting off and walking a bike up a steep hill became almost unthinkable.

And even that was the Dark Ages. In the 1980s, some bike boffin came up with the idea of adding cogs to the rear gear cluster. Suddenly bikes appeared with fifteen, eighteen even twenty-one and twenty-four gears. Mountain bikes appeared—ungainly hulks with great nubbly tires and complicated suspension systems. Serious cyclists debated the relative merits of brakes from Japan, sprockets from Italy and featherweight magnesium-alloy toe baskets from Czechoslovakia. My first bike, mint-fresh from the CCM factory, set my dad back a whopping $29.95. Today you can pay more than that for a pair of cycling gloves—and they won't even have fingers.

Or if you really want to wow your cycling friends the way Tommy Farmer wowed us way back in the fifties—buy yourself an Urbanite.

You can order one from Urbane Cyclist, a shop in Toronto. Urbanites sell for $750 per and they are cutting-edge trendy, with great colours, happening handlebars, a way cool imitation-leather saddle...

And oh, yes—no gears. The Urbanite is a single-speed bike, just like the ones the kamikaze bike couriers ride in the big city.

Just like the old CCM I learned to ride on half a century ago, as a matter of fact.

No difference really.

Aside from the $720.05.

DEAR DIARY: YOU MAKE ME SICK

I never travel without my diary. One should always have something sensational to read in the train.
—Oscar Wilde

Shows you how much difference a little talent can make. I've been keeping diaries for decades and the only time I reread them is when I'm having trouble falling asleep. My diaries are about as sensational as the Yellow Pages for Minot, North Dakota.

The trouble with diaries (well, with my diaries) is that they too quickly degenerate into a whiny litany of poor-little-me complaints and fatuous observations. Example? Here's an entry from my diary for Friday, October 18, 1988.

"3:58 p.m. Cloudy, mild. Waiting for the train in Union Station. Lost a pair of pigskin gloves this week, but found my favourite pair of reading glasses. Good trade. Besides, I found the gloves on a bus a year ago and they weren't that warm anyway…"

Trees died for this?

I guess if I had to defend my diarizing I'd argue that it gives me something to do in doctors' waiting rooms, coffee shops and airport lounges while other people are reading Harlequins, playing solitaire, filling in crosswords…or having a life.

Besides, it's supposed to be good for you, keeping a diary. Creative writing courses always stress the importance of carrying a notebook and jotting down your impressions. Motivational speakers recommend it as a daily habit.

And a lot of famous people have followed that advice. *Bridget Jones's Diary* became a movie. Virginia Woolf's diaries made her famous, and Mae West's made her rich. ("Keep a diary," said the legendary Hollywood gold digger, "and some day your diary will keep you.") And we would know a lot less of seventeenth-century life in London if an obscure secretary to the British Admiralty named Samuel Pepys hadn't scratched out daily observations in his diary.

Nevertheless, Dr. Elaine Duncan says they were all wasting their time and probably harming themselves to boot. Dr. Duncan, who is with Glasgow's Caledonian University, conducted a study of ninety-four students who kept diaries and compared their psychological profiles with forty-one students who didn't. "We expected diary-keepers to have some benefit, or be the same," she said, "but they were the worst off." Dr. Duncan speculated that by constantly writing about the negative events of their lives, diarists may never get over those events, resulting in various health disorders. The doctor's conclusion: "It's probably better not to get caught in a ruminative, repetitive cycle. You are probably much better off if you don't write anything at all."

Not that the Glasgow study will dampen the enthusiasm for diary keeping. In fact, thanks to computers and the internet, I reckon we're well into the Renaissance era for diaries. You know about blogging? That's where people type their thoughts, opinions, observations and all round blatherings into a computer and send them out over the internet for the delectation of the rest of us. Blogs are basically cyberdiaries.

Are they popular? Experts estimate that there are millions of blogs on the internet and the number is mushrooming by the hour. Blogs are so popular that Nokia, the world's largest mobile phone supplier, brought out a new cellphone to cater to the emerging market. It's called the Nokia 7610. It's about the size of a... well, diary, but it doesn't have pages. It has a large screen that can display photographs and even videos which bloggers can instantly send to all and sundry—via their cellphones.

It's got a name, this latest internet wrinkle—it's called life caching. A spokesman for Nokia describes it as "a new communications modality where people share their experiences on the Web and people who care about them read about it."

I call it...kind of sad. Researchers are just beginning to twig to the ironic Catch-22 of our love affair with the internet—the fact that even as it facilitates communication, productivity and information access, it withers face-to-face connection with family, friends, neighbours and the Korean guy who runs the corner store. Sure, I can bank online now, but it means I no longer get to hear about Alice the teller's kids or look at the local artwork in the credit union lobby.

Reminds me of something I saw the other day walking past a Toronto cybercafé full of people, all hunched over their individual keyboards, many of them tapping out their hopes and dreams, their fears and wonderings to...nobody really. To a void.

I wish I'd had the presence of mind to offer them an even more revolutionary communications modality. I wish I'd suggested they exit their programs, shut down their computers, turn to the person next to them and say, "Hi."

HOORAY FOR DUCT TAPE—WARTS AND ALL

I have a confession to make: I'm one of those guys who carries a Swiss Army knife on his belt.

You know the Swiss Army knife—a collection of not-quite-ready-for-prime-time minitools, all ingeniously welded onto a penknife. You get a bottle opener and a can opener, a nail file, a pair of tweezers, three or four screwdriver bits—and oh, yes, one or two knife blades.

That's on the classic model. If you want to go ultranerdy you can get the deluxe baby. It has pliers, a fish scaler, a compass, a ballpoint pen, two different saw blades and a toothpick. With top of the line models like that you get a leather carrying case for free.

There's no charge for the hernia either.

My Swiss Army knife falls in the mid-range. I opted to forgo the more esoteric bells and whistles, although I did insist on a model that has a toothpick—which turned out to be my most-used utensil.

But I've realized of late that I am just wasting my time, lugging around a Swiss Army knife. If I was truly interested in being a certified Handy Guy I would be carrying a roll of duct tape on my belt.

Sure! Good old shiny grey duct tape. You can fix way more things with a roll of over-the-counter duct tape than you can with any Swiss Army knife—or even with a Leatherman, (a much sturdier adaptation of the SAK—although tragically, sans toothpick). The astronauts on Apollo 13 saved their mission and probably their lives with a roll of duct tape. They used it to patch up some leaky carbon dioxide filters.

A multi-billion dollar enterprise rescued by a few cents worth of sticky tape.

I myself have used duct tape to put a splint on a ski pole, patch a hole in a canoe and hold a boot together for the last few miles of a hike. I've taped up gaping rents in tarpaulins, jerry-rigged tourniquets on garden hoses and saved myself from public embarrassment and possible arrest by conducting emergency repairs after the back seam of my trousers blew out during a game of pickup basketball in downtown Vancouver.

But any half-assed handyman can bend your ear for an hour on the merits of duct tape—heck, Red Green's up and made a movie about it. What I didn't know—and I'm sure even Red didn't know—is the amazing medical breakthrough for which we can now thank this humble household helper.

Duct tape gets rid of warts.

Really. Researchers at the Madigan Army Medical Center at Washington State University conducted an experiment in wart removal last year. They treated half their patients with the conventional wart therapy, which is to say they applied liquid nitrogen to the afflicted area and, in effect, burned the warts away. The other half got to wear a simple strip of duct tape over their warts for six days. At the end of that time they removed the tape, soaked the warts in water and sanded off the rough edges with emery boards.

Result: sixty percent of the patients treated with liquid nitrogen lost their warts—which is about what the doctors expected.

But an astounding eighty-six percent of the duct tape wearers found their warts were gone too.

Doctors aren't certain why duct tape works so well, but they theorize that the adhesive irritates the warts, possibly stimulating the immune system to attack the growths.

Best of all, duct tape is cheap—unlike liquid nitrogen. And painless—unlike liquid nitrogen. No doctor's appointment, no sitting in a waiting room twiddling your warty thumbs and reading 1998 issues of Maclean's magazine—just a quick trip to the Home Hardware followed by a little home doctorin'.

I don't personally have any home grown warts (if you exclude in-laws) but I remember having a couple on my left arm as a kid. I also remember reading about Tom Sawyer and his sure-fire cure for the ailment: rubbing a live toad on the afflicted area.

Not only is it faintly repulsive and highly disrespectful to the toad—it doesn't work.

Now maybe if I'd duct-taped that toad to my arm…

COME FLY WITH ME

Oh! I have slipped the surly bonds of Earth
And danced the sky on laughter-silvered wings...
—John Gillespie Magee, Jr.,"High Flight"

Tom Cochrane was right: life is a highway. What he forgot to mention is that it's also a one-way street. I have reached a stage of life in which a few blunt truths have made themselves painfully evident. There are certain things I've always dreamed of doing which, due to advancing decrepitude (mine), are simply not going to happen.

To wit:

Pat Quinn is not going to call me up to plug that hole in the Maple Leafs defensive corps.

The only way I'll ever see the summit of Mount Everest is on a *National Geographic* travelogue.

I can stop waiting for a late-night phone call from Jennifer Lopez complaining that she's lonely and would like to go out dancing.

And now I realize that I might as well give up on another long-nurtured dream.

I am never going to get to fly on the Concorde.

The obituaries for the Concorde briefly fluttered across the front pages of the national press and then, like the plane itself, were seen no more. The delta-winged supersonic luxury airliner was mothballed after barely a quarter-century of commercial service. The eulogies ranged from the rhapsodic, "Never before has such a beautiful object been designed and built by man," to the less charitable, "The largest, most expensive and most dubious project ever undertaken in the development of civil aircraft."

Beautiful? Well, I suppose so—although from some angles the Concorde looked like an albino praying mantis wearing a Batman cape—but she was unquestionably expensive. Only a handful of Concordes were ever built, but the price tag for development costs alone crested above $5 billion—and that's in 1960s dollars. More like $25 billion in today's currency.

And it's not like the plane ever made back its investment in passenger fares. It could only carry one hundred passengers per flight. By the time Concorde's owners pulled the plug, flights were running at twenty percent capacity. Which is to say four out of every five seats were empty.

Why? Pick your poison: ear cracking sonic booms, lingering air travel chill from 9/11, skyrocketing fuel prices, a spectacular crash into a Paris hotel that killed 109 people on the plane and four people on the ground...

And the relative scarcity of people willing and able to shell out roughly fifteen thousand loonies for a three-and-a-half hour jaunt from New York to Paris and back.

Truth is, the Concorde was an airborne white elephant. It never did have a lot of fans—just a few star-struck aviation big dreamers and a handful of wallet-heavy thrill-seekers—but it caught our attention for all that.

Sort of like Paris Hilton. And the Osbournes.

Still, the idea of the Concorde had its alluring charms for earthbound grunts like me. The thought of breakfasting on the Champs Élysées, hopping a cab to Charles de Gaulle airport, sipping champers and nodding to Sting, Diana Ross and Linda Evangelista over the finger foods at thirty-five thousand feet, then winding up at JFK just in time for lunch...

Yeah, that appeals to the unnourished sybarite in me.

But the truth is, I hate flying generally—whether it's a luxury airliner or a single-engine Beaver. Flying always makes my ears pop.

A stewardess told me that chewing gum would take care of that problem, so I bought a package of Dentyne and tried it.

It sort of worked.

But it took me days to get it out of my ears.

RUNNING ON EMPTY

Well, how about it—is the spiralling cost of gasoline driving you squirrelly? Are you about ready to take that high octane gasoline nozzle and stick it where the sun doesn't shine? Here's a heretical thought for you: we aren't paying *enough* at the pumps.

It's not my argument. It comes from the lips of William E. Rees, an economist and a professor at the University of British Columbia.

And I'm not sure he's wrong. What the professor has done is add up the hidden costs of each litre of gas we buy when we fill 'er up. The health costs, for instance, of all that pollution associated with the burning of fossil fuels. The environmental degradation. The millions of dollars our government forks over to the Big Oil Boys in the form of lavish subsidies and generous tax breaks. Professor Rees reckons that if we were really paying the freight, each litre of gas we buy would cost us anywhere from two bucks to five-forty a pop.

Maybe he's right. I do know that we humans have an ongoing love affair with our cars.

And we all know that love is blind.

A couple of years ago I visited the city of Florence, Italy. Florence is one of the great urban treasures on the planet. Unbelievable architecture. Breathtaking paintings and sculptures. Exquisite piazzas and galleries and streets.

I couldn't wait to get out of the place.

Florence…stinks. It is polluted with honking, spewing, farting vehicles that befoul the air, clog the lungs and befuddle the mind. If Michelangelo or Cellini or Giotto were to revisit their beloved metropolis, I know they would run screaming for the Tuscan hills. Dante would think he'd found his inferno. The internal combustion engine has turned Florence into a screeching, fume-shrouded, lung-searing urban nightmare.

Saddest thing of all, hardly anyone seems to notice.

It's a little different in Canada—we have more space—but we depend even more on the automobile. And the end result isn't any prettier. Rush hour in Vancouver or Montreal or Toronto isn't that different from rush hour in Rome, Paris or Singapore—it's still bloody awful.

Actually, if you've got a twisted sense of humour, it's ever so slightly hilarious. In London rush-hour traffic now moves more slowly than it did a hundred years ago when people travelled on foot and by horse.

Some places—in Western Europe particularly—are just beginning to fight back. Governments there are beginning to discern the obvious civic benefits (and municipal savings) of improved bus and streetcar systems and seriously dedicated bicycle lanes. Recently a hundred and fifty cities in France, Italy and Switzerland got together and agreed to ban automobiles completely for one day. Some cities, like Verona and Siena, have said to hell with it and banned cars entirely. In Paris a few months ago, more than two dozen government ministers showed up for a cabinet meeting riding bicycles and electric scooters.

Even Ottawa has made noises about kicking some money back into our national VIA Rail passenger service, which it's been quietly strangling for decades.

All of which makes our grousing and mewling about the price of gasoline faintly silly. Seventy-five cents a litre for gas got you down? That works out to what—two-fifty a gallon? Well, heads up, chum. You're also paying over five bucks a gallon for homogenized milk, eight bucks a gallon for orange juice and twenty-five bucks a gallon for Evian water.

Maple syrup will set you back more than fifty bucks a gallon—if you can find it at that price. Nope, when you think about it, gasoline's dirt cheap.

Or perhaps that should be…cheap and dirty.

KARAOKE? OKEY-DOKEY!

I remember the headline clearly. It read, "Karaoke Boom is Over."

I also remember my reaction clearly. It ran: And the downside to this news is…?

Karaoke, for anyone who's been living on Arcturus and thus fortunate enough to have missed it, is a phenomenon in which tone-deaf amateurs who've had too many beers are encouraged to get up in public and emulate singers with actual talent. This makes it possible for patrons to have their dinner or their private tête-à-tête interrupted by an accountant from Surrey caterwauling the half-remembered lyrics to "My Way" à la Sinatra.

Karaoke began—as did many ominous phenomena including Godzilla and Pokemon—in Japan. In 1971 a Japanese rock drummer who couldn't read a note of music hit upon the idea of bringing members of the audience up on stage and prodding them to sing along to popular song tracks.

Who could have guessed there were so many people out there who believed (erroneously) that they could sing? Karaoke swept across the globe like an influenza virus. In no time there were karaoke bars in Paris and Parry Sound, Moscow and Moosonee.

But the motherland—and the motherlode—for Madonna

wannabes and Elvis also-rans—continued to be Japan. The Japanese are traditionally a reserved and modest people, especially in public. Karaoke changed all that. The fad gave the Japanese the opportunity to shed their decorous shells and unleash their inner lounge crooners. They grabbed the opportunity—and the hand-held mike—with both hands and made karaoke the biggest thing in Japan since sushi.

Karaoke is big business in the Land of the Rising Sun. It generates more than $10 billion annually. There are half a dozen karaoke channels on Japanese cable TV. Japanese night schools offer courses in karaoke singing. And Japan doesn't just have smoky karaoke bars—it has karaoke mansions—huge, multi-storey edifices where hordes of patrons line up nightly to spend their money, drink their sake and sing their musically challenged tonsils off.

How many people? Well, bear in mind that, even in Japan, the karaoke business is in steep decline and has been for the past few years. Experts estimate that the number of karaoke singers has dropped by twenty percent since 1994.

And yet there are still forty-eight million Japanese who go out to karaoke bars and sing, on average, ten times a year.

Karaoke took off like disco, and it looks like it's about to flame out like disco too. It's taken two near-fatal hits in the past few years. First, a moribund Japanese economy that refuses to turn around is keeping would-be warblers out of the bars and close to home. Second, karaoke just ain't "in" anymore. Japanese teenagers regard karaoke as, well, dorky. Something dated and dopey that only their parents would consider doing in public.

Will it die out completely? I doubt it. Karaoke may be painful, pathetic and corny, but it's powerful. And there's enough sugar-cured ham in most of us to ensure that karaoke will always have the raw material to work with.

Because let's face it: most of us—right down to the last superannuated hippie—secretly believe we're couldabins. If I'd just learned a couple more guitar chords and spent the summer of '61 hanging out in Greenwich Village, I couldabin Bob Dylan. You couldabin Diana Krall if you'd stuck to the piano lessons and stayed away from the banana cream pie.

We just didn't get the breaks, is all.

In the meantime, the movers and shakers behind the karaoke phenomenon in Japan struggle to reinvent their golden egg-layer. Deep thinkers at Toyota, believe it or not, are lashing out big bucks to marry karaoke and driving. Some day soon we'll be treated to the sight of commuters stuck in traffic jams with one hand on the steering wheel and a cordless mike in the other, belting out "Born to Run" by Springsteen or "Beauty and the Beast" by Celine Dion.

Which is fine.

As long as they keep their windows rolled up.

MEASURE FOR MEASURE

By the time you read these words, Steve Thoburn could be in jail. But probably not. After all, he was convicted of his heinous crime way back in the year 2000 and despite the might and majesty of a hugely disapproving government, he's still walking free. Truth is, the government is just a teensy bit afraid of Steve Thoburn. And well they might be, for this is a man who—despite grave threats and dire promises of doom and perdition from the highest levels of authority—blissfully went ahead and...sold bananas.

Correction: Steve Thoburn sold bananas *by the pound.* And that's not allowed in the country Steve Thoburn calls home—which by the way, is not Nigeria or North Korea or some fly-blown Third World tin-pot dictatorship. Steve Thoburn is an Englishman—a greengrocer in Sunderland, to be precise. This makes him a citizen of the state that came up with the dictum "a man's home is his castle." But it also means he belongs to a member country of the European Common Market. And in the ECM, pounds and ounces are verboten. Sounds...well, Hitleresque. But the fact is, anytime a customer in Britain asks for goods in pounds and ounces, and the shopkeeper fails to measure the goods out in their metric equivalent, said shopkeeper is committing a criminal offence and is liable to jail time.

What complicates the problem is that every day that simple law is ignored, flouted and trampled in the Albion dust about ten million times. Brits are quite happy with their pounds and ounces, their fathoms and furlongs, their pecks and pints and quarts. Ninety percent of them strenuously oppose the idea of converting to metric. This is why the government tiptoes around Steve Thoburn and his old-time measuring scale. If they send him to jail, they'll have to do the same thing to virtually every shopkeeper in the country.

And Mr. Thoburn? He's no Jesse James. He's not even a Robin Hood. He is—in the country that Adam Smith called "a nation of shopkeepers"—a shopkeeper. He's just trying to satisfy the folks who buy his produce. Here's how he puts it:

"I object so strongly to this interference in the way I serve my customers just because of a law passed in another country by people we did not elect that I shall continue to sell in pounds and ounces if my customers want it. If I am prosecuted again, I will not pay any fine and they can put me in prison."

Don't know why the Brits don't just ask Canada for guidance. After all we've been flirting with the metric system since the 1970s. We've got thirty-odd years of hands-on metric experience over here. That's why today we live in a country where on your driver's licence your height is described in centimetres, but on a police APB it's in feet and inches. That's why we get to buy gas in litres for cars that are rated in miles per gallon. And live in houses that are measured in square feet, built on lots measured in square metres and erected with two-by-fours held together with three-inch nails.

My favourite morsel of metric measurement? The wind chill factor, which is now officially measured in watts per square metre. Yeah, that's useable.

My grocery store has two scales: one in kilos, the other in pounds and ounces. And good luck finding anyone on staff who can tell you whether 250 g will be enough for the quarter-pound of butter your cake recipe calls for. In my experience, the grocery clerks are just as confused as...well, I am.

Three decades on, what we have is a mishmash of weights and measures and millions of Canucks not quite sure just how far the next town is or how much that sack of potatoes weighs or how to brag about the fish we just caught ("Look, Maw—a 42 cm largemouth! Must run about 1.75 kg!").

I know the argument for metric: it's simpler and makes international trading easier. Well, that might be true if we'd actually adopted it—and if our major trading partner, the US, used it, which it doesn't.

The solution? Hey, who said anything about a solution? This is Canada, a country that's half French and half English, half European and half North American, half enthralled with the US and half terrified of it, half winter and half summer…Why shouldn't we have a system of weights and measures that's half metric and half imperial?

We're Canada, eh? Muddle is our middle name.

YOU TALKING TO *ME*, TOILET?

There were a couple of stories in the news last week that I'm still trying to wrap my head around. It's tough, because the stories pull my brain in opposite directions. The first item concerns the latest telephone innovation from our own beloved Bell Canada. While leading-edge communications giants like Nokia, Sony Ericsson and Toshiba continue to pump out tinier and tinier cellphones with more and more wireless features, Ma Bell is introducing…

The rotary telephone.

Yup, the big old clunky chunk of bakelite with the dial on the front and the curly cord that leads to a handset big enough to knock down a burglar. Rotary telephones were big back in the *Leave it to Beaver* era, then started to disappear in the seventies, replaced by touch-tone phones. Now they're making a comeback and it's hard to figure why. Rotary phones don't offer call waiting, call display, speakerphone or automatic redial but customers are clamouring for them anyway. "Some people have been asking for them and looking for them," says Bell Canada spokeswoman Gina Gottenburg, "so we thought we'd give our customers a choice of old or new."

What's the attraction? Nostalgia, I reckon. In a world where everything seems to change at warp speed, it might be comforting to have a substantial nugget of retro-tech you can actually hold in your hand. Lord knows not much else is safe from the cosmic stable-broom of change—not even the Swiss Army knife.

You know the Swiss Army knife? The Rolls-Royce of pocket knives. Most portable shivs feature one or two blades at most. The Swiss Army knife may have dozens, depending on the model. Not that they're all blades. My SAK has tweezers, two screwdrivers, a pair of miniscissors and several appendages I haven't figured out.

For my money, the Swiss Army knife is the perfect proto-gadget—an entire tool box that you can hold in your hand and wear on your hip. It's a perfectly sound piece of technological ingenuity that's been around for more than a century.

And now they've gone and computerized it.

I'm serious. Victorinox, which is the parent company, is now marketing a model they call the SwissMemory Army multi-tool. It looks like the old familiar red-shanked toad sticker except you can plug this one right into your computer. All you have to do is sidle up to a desktop or laptop, slot your SwissMemory "knife" into a USB port and you're set to download documents, photos, MP3 audio files, video files—whatever you need. Your handy-dandy SwissMemory has sixty-four megabytes of space to play with.

The deluxe SwissMemory also boasts scissors, a nail file, a screwdriver, a ballpoint pen, a flashlight—and a knife blade.

And good luck trying to jockey that baby past airport security.

I fear the SwissMemory multi-tool might be but the thin edge of the technological wedge. Some sadist somewhere has apparently decided that our machines need to be more interactive. Thus we have airport vending machines that try to seduce us into buying a Coke or a chocolate bar using a sexy, recorded robot voice.

Burghers in Berlin can look forward to talking trash cans next spring. The city fathers have okayed a plan to wire some of the city's twenty thousand public litter bins for sound. Users will hear a voice say "danke" when they toss their garbage in the bin. Some cans will also be programmed to say "thank you" and "merci" when their lids are popped—just to inject that soupçon of cosmopolitan flavour so lacking in conventional garbage collection…

It gets worse. In Amsterdam the toilets talk back to you. The owner of a popular café in central Amsterdam has installed motion sensors in his biffies that respond with a recorded message to the behaviour of folks using the facilities. Sometimes the toilet will chide you for not washing your hands. One visitor was told, "You might consider sitting down next time," in a sarcastic voice. Still another was warned that "the last visitor did not take heed of basic rules of hygiene." The toilets are also programmed to cough violently if somebody lights a cigarette and to expound on the futility of war and other weighty matters.

Who needs a lippy lavatory in his or her life? Well, the creator—one Leonard van Munster— claims his talking toilets are "an artistic statement." He even threatens to build more "if the demand arises."

I wouldn't hold my breath on that one, Leonard. And if I ever catch you installing sensors on my throne, I'll clock you upside the head. With my rotary phone.

KEEP IT SIMPLE, STUPID

I see that WestJet is planning to put seat-back televisions in all its airplanes. As an aircraft user and confirmed fan of the airline, may I offer a word of advice?

Don't.

Seat-back televisions on airplanes are a bad idea for WestJet. Just like the leather seats they've started putting in their planes. And those newfangled head rests that supposedly contour to the passenger's head.

WestJet is getting fancy, and fancy isn't their strong suit. The Calgary-based company became successful as the no-frills airline. People flocked to the WestJet ticket counter not because they wanted TV sets or leather seats or high-tech headrests. They wanted cheap flights. And WestJet delivered. Recently I had to fly from Victoria to Thunder Bay return. Air Canada wanted more than twenty-one hundred dollars to do the job. WestJet got me there and back for a little over eight hundred dollars. WestJet made itself the Volkswagen Beetle of the skies and quickly became the most profitable airline in the country. Now it's tinkering with the very formula that made it a success. If they keep it up they'll be as snooty and insolvent as That Other Airline in no time.

What is it about the human animal that compels us to constantly fix things that work fine until we ensure that they don't? Take the bicycle. There was a time when everybody rode simple, one-speed bikes with nice soft seats and fat, cushiony tires. They were cheap and durable and they lasted forever.

Today the average bike has anywhere up to twenty-five speeds. It's made of space-age magnesium-titanium alloys and runs on tires that slew perfectly into sewer grates. It has shock absorbers, a sophisticated braking system and a Rube Goldbergish derailleur rig that breaks down more often than Liza Minnelli. Oh, yeah, and it costs a king's ransom to boot.

Curt Harnett and Lance Armstrong need bikes like that. You and I would be fine with a CCM one-speed.

And razors. I happen to believe that one of the great inventions of the twentieth century was the disposable razor. Unlike the noisy, expensive and inefficient electric model, the disposable razor is safe, quiet, cheap and recyclable. So what's Gillette doing to the disposable?

Putting a battery in it.

Welcome to the M3 Power Razor. It's got a slot in the handle for an AAA battery, which, Gillette says, provides "a gentle, pulsing action" which supposedly lifts whiskers for a closer shave. Price for the M3 kit? $19.99. Which is about ten times more than I pay for a six-pack of BIC disposables.

Wasn't broken, Gillette. Didn't need fixing.

But then there's LG Electronics. This company is to Gillette Razors as Microsoft is to Mississippi mud wrestling. LG Electronics has just unveiled its latest brainwave: the internet refrigerator.

The new fridge has a cyclopean computer screen on the front panel and a touch pad allowing users to, for instance, connect to a database of three hundred recipes, searchable by ingredient. Don't have the two ounces of smoked Gruyère the recipe calls for? *No problemo*. You can order the ingredients from an online grocer, right from your refrigerator. The LG Internet Refrigerator (hereafter referred to as Hal) will also remind you when the celery is wilting and the meat loaf in the far back corner is growing green fur.

There's a built-in camera, of course, in case you want to leave a video message for the kids. Oh, yes…and you can watch TV on Hal and play downloaded MP3s through its speakers.

"It's really a communications centre," burbles Frank Lee, the firm's online marketing manager. "The kitchen is the centre of the home, so this makes sense."

Perhaps to a cyborg, Frank. And a rich cyborg at that. The LG behemoth retails for $11,999.

Maybe I'm a curmudgeon, but I find it increasingly difficult to watch TV in the comfort of my living room, never mind standing at my refrigerator. And the day I hear P. Diddy emanating from my vegetable crisper is the day I pull the plug and go back to an icebox.

Remember the advice of Horace, the Roman poet who lived and wrote a couple of millennia ago: "Avoid greatness. In a cottage there may be more real happiness than kings or their favourites enjoy."

Amen. And if you throw in an icebox, you'll be living in paradise.

PART IV:
ONLY HUMAN

THE WAR BETWEEN THE SEXES

Men and women, women and men. It will never work
—Erica Jong

There's a brand new babysitting service available in Hamburg, Germany. For ten Euros—that's about eighteen bucks Canadian—housewives bent on shopping can drop off their charges at the Nox Bar in downtown Hamburg. The deposit buys the women a few uninterrupted hours in the shops and boutiques, while their "responsibilities" are treated to two beers, a meal and unlimited televised sports on the big screens mounted over the bar.

Obviously we're not talking about the ladies' offspring here. We're talking about their mates. Men hate shopping, and women hate shopping with a grumpy spouse in tow. Solution: park him in a sports bar and everybody's happy.

It's a kindergarten for grownups—male grownups specifically. It's also a graphic illustration that men indeed are from Mars, women are from Venus and seldom will their intergalactic orbits intertwine.

We really are different, you know. Screw all that Alan Alda, sensitive-caring-male bushwa. Men and women are like the poles of a magnet—constantly pushing in equal but opposite directions.

My partner recently went away on a trip for ten days. I knew there'd be trouble when she got back. Sure enough. Not two minutes in the door and she's muttering about a few empty pork and bean tins on the kitchen counter, whiskers in the bathroom sink and a high-tide mark on the bathtub that looks like one of the rings of Saturn. Talk about neurotic.

It pains me to say this, but women just aren't very practical. Why should I make the bed every morning when I know perfectly well I'm just going to have to unmake it at the end of the day? What's the point of wasting a valuable resource like hot water to do dishes morning, noon and night when I can just let them pile up and do them all in one marathon session Saturday afternoon? Okay, Saturday afternoon and evening? Why doesn't *everyone* hang his undershorts on the lampshade if he knows he's going to wear them the next day? It makes them easy to find, plus they're warm when you put them on.

In any case, it's not my fault. I have an untreatable medical condition. I'm a man. That means that, besides having two or three gender-specific anatomical doodads, I am mentally programmed differently from women. All men are, according to Michael Gurian. He's a social philosopher and he's just published a book called *What Could He Be Thinking?: How a Man's Mind Really Works.*

Gurian says my brain simply doesn't take in sensory details as efficiently as a woman's. In other words, it's not that I'm a slob, I literally do not *see* that smear of peanut butter on the fridge door or yesterday's balled-up sweat socks draped across the chesterfield.

I'm at a chemical disadvantage too. Gurian claims that the male brain secretes only a tiny dribble of a powerful bonding chemical called oxytocin. Women's brains are awash in the stuff. Oxytocin deprivation explains why men shy away from touchy-feely conversations. Also why most of us would prefer a prostate exam conducted by a doctor wearing a hockey glove over the ordeal of sitting through one edition of Oprah.

And oxytocin isn't the only chemical we get shortchanged on. Gurian says men also produce less serotonin than women, which is why we need more of what he calls "mindless" distractions to relax, like "Monday Night Football" and Schwarzenegger flicks.

Does Gurian expect his book to change male pattern dumbness? No, he sees no future there. His book is an attempt to help women better understand the Homer Simpson in their life. "Men get this already," says Gurian. "They are living this brain, but they don't have the conscious language to explain it."

Oh, I don't know. I thought George Burns nailed it pretty good. He said, "There will always be a battle between the sexes because men and women want different things.

"Men want women and women want men."

OF ALL THE NERVE!

One of the strengths of the English language is that when it doesn't have a decent homegrown word, it imports as necessary from foreign tongues. One of our great imports is chutzpah. It comes from Yiddish and means "supreme self-confidence." Nerve, gall.

And a little bit more.

Michelle Landsberg, a columnist for the *Toronto Star*, used to live in New York city. She wrote a book called *This Is New York, Honey*! The title came from something that happened to her on Park Avenue one afternoon. Landsberg had hailed a taxi and opened the back door and was about to climb in when she was blindsided, cross-checked and left on the curb by a well-dressed matron who deftly wedged herself into the cab and started barking instructions to the driver.

"B-b-b-but I hailed this taxi," objected Landsberg. The interloper fixed her with a deadpan stare and snarled, "This is New York, honey!" as the taxi sped away.

That's chutzpah.

But you don't have to live in New York to encounter the phenomenon. O.J. Simpson was in the news a while back, musing about how he'd like to try his hand as a news commentator—on the then-upcoming trial of alleged actor-murderer Robert Blake.

"I think I have a lot of insight," said Simpson—also an alleged actor-murderer. That's chutzpah. If Fox News had signed him up, that would be chutzpah squared.

There's a Swazi radio correspondent who seems to have a fair dose of the condition as well. This guy was providing live daily reports from Baghdad during the 2002 Saddamectomy. He was one of the very few correspondents willing to risk their lives to be at the centre of the attack as the American maelstrom descended.

At least, that's what his radio listeners thought. Turns out he was broadcasting from a broom closet in downtown Johannesburg.

And let's not forget Sinéad O'Connor in the chutzpah sweepstakes. The Irish thrush-cum-flake, famous for shredding a picture of the Pope on stage, has announced that she is retiring from show business. "I request that as of July, since I no longer seek to be a famous person, and instead I wish to live a normal life, could people please afford me my privacy," she wrote.

On her website.

Hey, Sinéad—no problem here. I won't call if you don't call.

No report on chutzpah would be complete without some input from the legal profession. I nominate Manhattan lawyer Jeffrey Powell. He recently sued singer-songwriter John Fogerty for US $5 million as compensation for "profound loss of hearing in his left ear." Seems Mr. Powell went to a music concert featuring Mr. Fogerty and found the music too loud.

Alas, Mr. Powell's plaints fell on deaf ears. An unsympathetic judge pointed out that "an objective, reasonable, 56-year-old lawyer" should be smart enough to intuit that voluntarily purchasing a ticket to a rock concert might conceivably lead to loud music causing hearing impairment. He threw the case out.

Give your head a shake, Mr. Powell. Might clear that left ear.

Any Canadian chutzpah candidates? Or are we just too bland, diffident and polite in the Great White North to play in the brass balls big leagues?

Meet Dustin Dickeson, of Sechelt, BC. He's twenty-three years old now but he's got more mileage on his odometer than the average twenty-three-year-old. Back when he was seventeen, Dickeson had an affair with his high school accounting teacher. Word got out, the ordure hit the air-circulating device, the teacher was canned and Dickeson was protected by a court-ordered publication ban.

Well, Dickeson went to court to get the ban lifted. Seems he's graduated—into a self-styled gangsta rapper, complete with a home-pressed CD. "I got stuff coming up in New York," he explained to a provincial court judge. That's why he wanted the publication ban removed. He wanted to cash in on his notoriety.

Traumatized by the event? Not hardly. There's a song on his CD called "Teacher's Scandal," which features the tender lyric "the bitch couldn't resist my charm."

Sounds to me like Dustin Dickeson is ready for New York.

If he'll promise to take out citizenship, I'll kick in for bus fare.

WARNING! KINDNESS AHEAD!

No act of kindness, no matter how small, is ever wasted.

A Greek chap by the name of Aesop scratched that observation down on parchment about twenty-five centuries ago. It is a simple gem, as verities go. Self-evident. I've never heard—can't imagine—anyone disputing it.

And I don't know anyone, with the possible exception of the Dalai Llama, who even pretends to live by it.

Well, him and the Kindness Crew.

The Kindness Crew is Val Litwin, Chris Bratseth, Erik Hanson and Brad Stokes—four twenty-something Victoria lads who recently crossed the country in a psychedelic motor home committing random acts of kindness wherever they parked.

What sort of acts? Oh, they showed up at SPCA kennels offering to wash and exercise the animals. They made sandwiches and handed them out to work crews on construction sites. They treated homeless people to hot meals, went shopping for shut-ins, entertained patients at a kids' hospital, fixed flats, weeded gardens, swept city streets, picked up hitchhikers, drove old-age pensioners to the bank and handed out free hugs to grumpy bus passengers.

And the fee was always the same. Nada. Nil. Zilch.

I met these guys in Vancouver earlier when they were merely talking about their cross-Canada odyssey. Cynical observer that I am, I tried to figure out their angle. Here were four healthy-looking white kids who looked like they could be modelling college fashions for the Bay's catalogue. Instead they were planning to travel from sea to sea doing good deeds, like superannuated boy scouts. Why? They were not Mormons or Scientologists or Jehovah's Witnesses or even Catholics. They were not spoiled rich kids working on a high-tech PhD thesis.

I reckoned they were good for two weeks of hard travelling before they'd limp back to Victoria and forget the whole thing.

I was wrong. As I write, they are close to halfway across the country, moving out of Regina and onto Winnipeg. They've still got Ontario, Quebec, the Maritimes and Newfoundland to go. They plan to wrap up their tour in, fittingly enough, one of Canada's friendliest cities—St. John's.

Adventures? They've had a lifetime's worth already, from blowing minds in downtown Vancouver—as they Windexed office building windows and swept the streets with whisks and dustpans—to riding wild horses in Merritt, BC. That's where a cowboy said, "You wanna perform an act of kindness, pardner? Great. Whyncha bust this bronco for me?"

And they did.

Well. At least they didn't get trampled.

And already they've noticed a curious thing on what they are calling the Extreme Kindness Tour. It's becoming apparent that random acts of kindness are contagious. People along the way keep showing up at their motorhome with urns of coffee and baked goodies for them. They get "adopted" by families who keep taking them home for dinner. Four guys who set out to be kind to others are drowning in kindnesses returned to them. If you check their website (www.extremekindness.com) you'll note that they write more about being grateful for kindness received than they do about kindness dispensed.

Even hard-headed businessmen have caught the virus. The Extreme Kindness Tour has picked up corporate sponsors ranging from a hotel chain to a footwear manufacturer.

Still, you have to wonder about these guys. What would possess four normal Canadian kids to spend three months of their lives doing menial chores for strangers?

It's no big mystery to the Kindness Crew. They have a simple mantra: inspiration, motivation, stimulation, kind-to-the-nation.

They had alternatives. They could be spending their twenties in a fog of keg parties, fast cars, smoky poolrooms and dumb television like…er…someone I once knew.

The philosopher Jean-Jacques Rousseau wrote, "What wisdom can you find that is greater than kindness?" Good question.

Another good question: why a random acts of kindness tour?

Why not?

WATCH YOUR LANGUAGE!

In certain trying circumstances, profanity furnishes a relief denied even in prayer.
—Mark Twain

Old Mr. Twain knew whereof he spake. The creator of Tom Sawyer and Huckleberry Finn was, of course, a master of exquisitely phrased English, but he was also no slouch when it came to calling a spade a spade.

Or a @#%*^& shovel, if he felt the situation warranted. As a matter of fact, Twain was so adept at colourful language that his wife was embarrassed. She tried various approaches to clean up his conversation.

One morning Twain cut himself shaving and cursed a blue streak at the top of his lungs. When he was done, his wife decided to shame him by repeating, calmly and dispassionately, every profanity that had spilled from her husband's lips.

Twain listened calmly, then observed, "You have the lyrics, my dear, but I'm afraid you'll never master the melody."

I can't help but wonder what Mr. Twain would make of the predicament Timothy Boomer finds himself in. Mr. Boomer will be going to trial soon. And if he loses his case, he could well be going to jail.

His offence? Swearing. Last summer the twenty-four-year-old automotive engineer rented a canoe with some friends during a vacation in northern Michigan. Mr. Boomer, evidently a better engineer than canoeist, paddled his craft straight onto a rock, whereupon the canoe tipped, depositing Mr. Boomer into the Rifle River.

At which point Mr. Boomer bemoaned his fate in salty language loud enough to catch the ears of three county sheriffs who were patrolling the waterways looking for underage drinkers.

The law enforcement officers, cognizant of the fact that there was, as they put it, "a mother with her kids within earshot," pulled Mr. Boomer out of the water, then slapped him with a citation for using "indecent, immoral, obscene, vulgar or insulting language in the presence of women or children."

It sounds a tad archaic, but there's nothing antiquated about the penalty the citation carries. Timothy Boomer's dirty mouth could get him ninety days in a Michigan jail.

I don't know exactly what words Mr. Boomer uttered, but they couldn't be much fouler than the stuff I can tune into on late night TV—or overhear walking by the local schoolyard, for that matter.

Cussing ain't what it used to be—and I think the world is poorer for it. When I was a kid, you could get yourself thrown out of school for using the word "damn." When my grade eleven English teacher, reading *Oliver Twist* to the class, came to the part where Mr. Bumble says, "The law is a ass…" the whole class giggled uncontrollably.

How innocent that seems now.

You don't realize it when you live day in and day out with words, but they have a shelf life—just like bread or milk. A word that makes you blush today can sound silly a few years from now. Two hundred years ago, the filthiest epithets you could fling were "Gadzooks!" and "Zounds!"

The words were purest blasphemy. "Gadzooks" was a corruption of "God's hooks," referring to the nails that held Christ to the cross. Similarly "zounds" was a corruption of "his wounds," the ones caused by "God's hooks."

"Bloody" is a fairly bland adjective to apply these days —"I can't find the bloody car keys!"—but it wasn't always. "Bloody" is a compressed version of "By Our Lady"—referring to Mary, Mother of God.

Not something you'd want to let fly in front of the parish priest.

I'm sorry to be living in a time when swear words are losing their lustre—becoming so commonplace—not because I'm offended by salty lingo; on the contrary. I think good solid swear words are the spice of language. But in cooking and in talking, when you use too many spices, all you do is kill the taste buds. The secret of spices—and swearing—is rationing.

The story is told of US President Harry S. Truman referring to an opponent's speech as "nothing but a bunch of horse manure."

It was suggested to his wife Bess that she persuade her husband to tone down his language. After all, it wasn't fitting to hear a president of the United States talk about "horse manure."

Mrs. Truman rolled her eyes and replied, "You don't know how long it took me to tone it down to 'horse manure!'"

LOTTERIES—YOU'VE GOTTA LOTTO LOSE

Not long ago a Quebec woman wrote a book about becoming a multi-millionaire. She was qualified—she had picked the winning ticket in a provincial lottery and scooped up several million greenbacks.

She reckons it was just about the worst thing that ever happened to her.

Before the win she was an average, middle-class Québécoise—she had a decent home, a husband, a job and lots of friends. She has none of those now.

She quit her job, of course—isn't that what all nouveau millionaires do first thing? Next she sold her dinky little house and bought a sprawling mansion more befitting to her millionaire status. Then the calls started coming in. Not just from relatives and neighbours—from folks she'd barely met and often hadn't seen in decades. They all loved her dearly, of course. Had always admired her and delighted in her good fortune—and wondered if she could see her way clear to sharing a paltry few thousand from her huge winnings. She was besieged by hundreds of supplicants, all of whom adored her no end.

Until she turned them down and immediately became Madame Rich Bitch—too good for her former peers.

But she had other problems by now. The new money had caused her husband to blossom into a Wall Street junkie. He appropriated huge chunks of the lottery money and shovelled it into the stock market.

He lost it all and burned up what was left of the marriage in the process.

Swiftly, weasel ratbag lawyers sank their hollow fangs into the estate siphoning off what was left of her windfall. She lost the mansion and now lives in a tiny walk-up, hoping that her book sells enough copies to pay the rent. Her one piece of advice to any lottery winner? Leave home immediately for at least one year—no forwarding address.

Winning the lottery can swiftly turn into a curse. A factory worker in Gateshead, England, recently won more than ten million in a lottery. He was very generous with his newfound loot. He bought seven grand houses on the same street in Gateshead and gave them all to family members so that they could all live next to one another.

That was two years ago. All those houses are for sale now. The lottery winner and his family have moved to New Zealand. Why? Perhaps it was a result of that brand new Honda Accord being firebombed in his sister's driveway. More likely it was a decision reached after persons unknown poured gasoline all over the porch of his brand new house and tried to set it alight.

Who would do that—and why? Who knows? A neighbour says, "The attacks on the family are disgraceful. They are perfectly nice people. Someone must be jealous of their wealth."

I feel for them both—the English and the Quebec lottery winner. But to tell the truth, I also feel the teensiest bit smug. I know that I will never be in their shoes because I will never win a lottery.

I don't buy lottery tickets. One of the few truths I know about myself is that I definitely lack the character to be an instant millionaire.

Call me unimaginative, but I actually need the pressure of mortgage payments, hydro bills and the hulking shadow of an insatiable Revenue Canada to keep me on the straight and narrow. Put a cheque for a million bucks in my hand and it would take about three nanoseconds to turn me into an instant libertine. Three thousand dollar hand-tailored suits. A stretch limo—three stretch limos—in the driveway. Oh, yeah. I'd be phoning up Harrods for takeout fried hummingbird tongues with one hand and urinating on my boss's desk with the other.

And of course I'd blow it all. And cheese off all my buddies and loved ones into the bargain. I'm not strong enough to survive a lottery win. Not like Gerald Swan. Mr. Swan, of Orton, Ontario, recently won the Heart and Stroke Foundation jackpot—one million bucks. His plans for the money?

He's going to give it away. All of it. "I'm quite comfortable the way I am," he says. "I don't need it. I bought the ticket because it's a good cause. God gave me this gift; I should give it back."

And he has. Gerald Swan has handed over the money to the Heart and Stroke Foundation, the Canadian Cancer Society and a camp for children with kidney disease.

Gerald Swan—a class act. He may not die with a lot of money in the bank, but I'm betting he dies with a smile on his face.

LOVE IS BLONDE

It was a blonde. A blonde to make a bishop kick a hole in a stained glass window.
—Raymond Chandler

It isn't that gentlemen really prefer blondes, it's just that we look dumber.
—Anita Loos

The most common unsolicited bit of data I get in my email (not counting the guaranteed penis enlargement ads and that guy in Nigeria who wants to use my bank account to deposit US $45 million) would have to be dumb blonde jokes. I get at least a dozen a week. Friends pass them onto me. They pop up unbidden on other peoples' websites.

There was even an inadvertent dumb blonde joke in the style section of the *Washington Post* last week. According to a World Health Organization study, the story claimed, women with blonde hair are (you'll excuse the pun) dying out, because men prefer mating with fake blondes. The story even made it on to the major US networks including CBS, where überblonde Diane Sawyer wailed that she and her ilk were on the endangered species list and in danger of "going the way of the snail darter."

Cute story. Too bad it wasn't true. Turns out there was no such study from the World Health Organization. The whole thing was an internet put-on perpetrated by an anonymous German hacker in Düsseldorf.

Still, it does speak to humankind's eternal bedevilment over women with yellow hair.

It's an obsession that doesn't carry over in the animal world, curiously enough. Palominos don't get extra points in the horse world; as for dogs, golden labs aren't any more special than their black brethren.

And when it comes to lions, it appears that brunettes rule. Researchers claim that female lions prefer steadies with dark, shoulder-length shrubbery. For the male, a longer and darker mane means more groupies—and more clout. Other male lions are intimidated by the dark-haired types, and if it comes to a scrap, the paler Leos usually lose.

Scientists know all this, thanks to a dirty trick perpetrated in Serengeti National Park in Tanzania last year. That's where Dr. Craig Packer, an animal behaviourist and student of lions for the past twenty-five years, set up several pairs of life-sized, dark-maned dummy male lions and sat back with a clipboard to chart reactions from real lions in the area.

Basically the reactions were two-fold and gender-specific: the male lions were spooked; the female lions were horny.

"The males were jittery and pussy-footed up to the toy carefully," says Packer, "but the females saw the male as advertising how sexy he was, and the females can be very sexy in response to these toys."

"It's embarrassing to watch a female offer herself up to a toy and be rejected."

And, says Dr. Packer, the darker the mane on the dummy, the more extreme the reaction.

Whereas with humans it seems to be exactly the reverse. Consider Courtney Love. The thirty-something rocker is a big, brassy blonde and proud of it. "Being blonde is a massive cultural responsibility," she says.

"I like to think of blondes as the knights in chess. It's what makes chess complicated. Knights are the first piece you look at—they elevate the game.

"No chess master wants to lose her knights. Blondes are the same: Without us, you cannot win, and you've got no one to blame for complicating everything."

Not that being blonde is a total cakewalk. Love points out that as a blonde "you have way more power than the other women in the room, but you have to take your punishment as well. Your sexual availability goes up, and your IQ drops below 110. Bank loans will be harder."

Maybe that's why dumb blonde jokes are so popular—because blondes are so powerful they scare the rest of us.

But real pros know how to roll with the punches. As Dolly Parton says, "I don't worry about dumb blonde jokes because I know I'm not dumb.

"Of course, I'm also not blonde."

NAME YOUR POISON

The late great Marshall McLuhan once said that a man's name is a numbing blow from which he never recovers. Maybe that's true. And maybe that's why so many folks up and change their birth names. Some handle switchers do it for obvious reasons. Vanity. Embarrassment. Ambition. Tony Curtis looks better on a marquee than Bernie Schwartz. And who's going to line up to see a celluloid cowboy with a moniker like Marion Morrison? Nobody, figured Marion. So he changed his name to John Wayne.

Occasionally entire metropolises change their names. Ontario used to have a town named Berlin until, in a fit of anti-German patriotism, the citizens redubbed it Kitchener. And but for an impassioned plea from the British writer Rudyard Kipling, we would have lost Medicine Hat, Alberta. "It is a lawful, original, sweat-and-dust-won name," wrote Kipling, "and to change it would be to risk the luck of the city, to disgust and dishearten old-timers...and to advertise abroad the city's lack of faith in itself."

Just as well Kipling's jeremiad carried the day. The citizens of Medicine Hat were thinking of changing the name of the place to Gasburg.

Musicians come up with some truly loopy name changes. Arnold Dorsey was a London lounge singer whose career was going nowhere—

until he changed his name to Englebert Humperdinck. Go figure.

And the singer Yusuf Islam can't seem to make up his mind. He calls himself Yusuf now, but his birth name was Stephen Georgiou. Although if you've got any grey in your thatch at all, you'll remember him better as Cat Stevens.

We won't even touch on the pretentious fop who insisted that he be addressed as The Artist Formerly Known As Prince.

But you don't have to be musical to be nominally nutsoid. Consider the case of Zdravkov Levichov. He is—was—a Bulgarian construction worker, but an unhappy one. Until he exchanged the name he was born with for that of an English soccer club. "I've always been a Manchester United fan," he explained to a reporter from the *Edinburgh Scotsman*, "and I've wanted to change my name ever since I was a schoolboy. But under communism it was not possible."

Bulgaria became democratic in 1990, and Zdravkov became Manchester United shortly thereafter—but his fight isn't over. The Bulgarian courts have ruled that his new legal name is Manchester Zdravkov Levichov United. Manny says he won't rest until the two middle names are history.

Could be weirder. We could be in Lake City, Florida, where "God" lives. "God" is Charles Haffey—or at least Charles wishes he was. A Columbia Circuit Court judge turned down Haffey's request to change his name to "God" but they reached a compromise. Now Charles Haffey is official known as "I am who I am."

"My first name, of course, will be 'I am,'" explained Mr.....er, Who I Am.

Ah, yes. Names can be confusing. And sometimes it comes down to a single letter. Take the case of Luciano Buonocore of Gragnano, Italy.

Or maybe it's Luciana.

That's what it says on his birth certificate. A simple spelling mistake in the maternity ward turned into a lifetime of mistaken-sex misery for Luciano. For the next twenty-eight years he was officially classified as a female. He couldn't get a national identity card. He was hassled over his driver's licence. He wasn't allowed to enlist in the army. Now he's engaged to be married—and he's not sure if he can, because to the Italian state, Luciano is still officially a woman and Italy doesn't recognize same-sex unions.

Not surprisingly, Luciano-Luciana has rather firm views on the naming of children. "I don't know exactly what I'll name my kids," he says. "But I'll sure take the birth certificates to a lawyer."

The famous movie mogul Sam Goldwyn had strong views about names too. When an assistant told Sam he was going to name his newborn infant Arthur, Sam exploded.

"Don't name the kid Arthur! Every Tom, Dick and Harry is named Arthur!"

NUDES IN THE NEWS

I see my good friend Judy Williams is in the news again.

Well, maybe not "good friend." We only got together once for about an hour.

Mind you, we were both naked at the time.

Judy does that a lot—hangs around in the buff, I mean. She's the Canadian rep for the International Naturist Action Committee. She's also spokeswoman for Skinny-Dippers Nude Recreation, a group that likes to get together of an evening at a public swimming pool in Surrey, BC, shuck their duds and frolic, sans benefit of Jantzens.

Used to like to get together and do that. Surrey city council has pulled the plug on their unadorned get-togethers by denying pool-rental rights to the group, even though the skinny dippers have been renting the pool once a month for half a year.

So what happened—whitewater orgies in the shallow end? Hordes of squinty old guys in stained raincoats clogging up the spectators' gallery?

Nah. Nothing happened. The nude swims were always closed to the public anyway, and—news flash for Surrey city council—nudists are not what you'd call a high-flying, party-down kind of people. By and large, they are as sedate and non-threatening as your Aunt Marge at a strawberry social. The participants in the Surrey skinny dip were mostly family types and group members ranging in age from eight months to eighty-eight years. One lifeguard says that "the nudies" were the pool's best-behaved customers.

What probably happened is what usually occurs when civic authorities come up against the idea of naked human bodies being exposed in public—the civic authorities freaked and fell all over themselves in a rush to throw a blanket over the whole situation.

Typically, city council members Don't Want To Talk About It. They've refused to talk to the media and they won't meet with Judy Williams to explain their actions.

They're probably terrified that she'll show up naked.

She might too. Judy is an avowed and unabashed nudist. In the summer months she spends as much of her spare time as possible avoiding tan lines on Vancouver's famous Wreck Beach.

Wreck Beach, in case you haven't heard, is a "clothing optional" recreational venue. Actually, it would be a brave soul who would venture onto the beach with clothes on. The naked denizens would hoot and razz you right back into the trees.

Back when I had a radio show on CBC, I heard about Judy Williams and decided I wanted to interview her. I called her up. Would she be willing to come to the studio? No, she said, would I be willing to bring my microphone and tape recorder to Wreck Beach? I agreed. She told me to meet her at such and such an entrance at twelve noon sharp. "Oh, and one more thing," she said. "Be naked. I will be."

Judyjudyjudy. Where were you when I was a hormone-besotted youth in high school?

It was a lovely spring day as I recall. The sun was shining, the seagulls were mewling, the sailboats were scudding across the bay and I was standing there, in front of Judy Williams, dressed only in a ball cap and a Sony tape recorder.

And what did Judy Williams look like? Was she a brazen temptress? A *Playboy* centrefold? A Salome? Naw. She looked like your kid's grade three teacher, or the current accounts teller down at the credit union. Except with no clothes on.

And how did it feel to be butt-naked in amongst acres of butt-naked sun worshippers? It felt...grand. Eventually. Oh, initially there was much folding of arms and flapping of hands and crossing of legs, but gradually you realize that naked human bodies en masse are about as erotic as a convention of plumbing contractors.

Besides, Wreck Beach is nothing if not egalitarian. It features tall folks, short folks, old and young and fat and skinny folks. Doesn't take long to figure out that you really have nothing to hide, so you might as well let it all hang out. Everybody else is.

That's what I learned from my day at the beach with Judy Williams, that the sense of shame about naked bodies which is drilled into us as kids is...well, a shame, really. Nakedness is no big deal.

As Donald Sutherland found out on his first meeting with Tallulah Bankhead. Sutherland was putting on makeup in his dressing room when he heard a noise behind him. He turned around to see Tallulah standing there, stark naked.

"What's the matter, dah-ling?" she asked. "Haven't you ever seen a blonde before?"

EARTH TO PRUDES: LIGHTEN UP

Marshall McLuhan once said something to the effect that no goldfish ever was aware that it lived in a goldfish bowl—point being that none of us can know what or who we are until we manage to step outside our environment and look back at it. That's why that famous space photo of planet Earth—all blue and green and white and swirling—was so electrifying. We'd never seen ourselves from outside our global fishbowl.

It makes me wonder if people of the Victorian Age ever realized that they were... well, Victorian. Prudish. Uptight. Laughably hypersensitive about sex and mores.

Makes me wonder if anybody realizes we're doing it again.

We're getting pretty silly, folks. Cynthia Stewart, a Cleveland housewife, may well be on her way to the slammer. Her crime? Well, she'd taken a roll of film into her local drugstore for development. A photo clerk there took one look at some of the shots on the roll and called the cops. The cops moved in and charged Mrs. Stewart with "pandering sexually oriented material involving a minor." Sure enough, on the film are shots of an eight-year-old female rinsing off after a bath using a detachable shower spray. One minor thing about the minor—she is Cynthia Stewart's daughter. "Throughout her life I have taken pictures of her to record the growth of her body and moments of silliness and play," Ms. Stewart testified. She has been suspended without pay from her job as a school bus driver and faces up to sixteen years in prison if convicted.

I am reminded of that Coppertone ad—you know the one, where a mutt on the beach is pulling down a little waif's bathing suit bottom and the (gasp!) cleft of her bum is showing? Sure hope they nail the Madison Avenue pervert responsible for that one.

The folks railroading Ms. Stewart would feel right at home in the town of Fall River, Nova Scotia. Authorities there recently suspended three grade-schoolers for the heinous crime of "snowing." Snowing is when kids…run around in the snow and push each other into snowbanks. It is also known as "fun."

Except at Georges P. Vanier Junior High School in Fall River. That's where a teacher last winter noted "suspicious" signs of snow on a young girl's jacket and reported her to the principal. Yes, the kid admitted, they (three girls and a boy, all close friends) had been frolicking in the snow. At George P., that qualifies as aggressive behaviour.

No one had been hurt. None of the kids had complained. They were all suspended.

Does it get stupider than this?

Actually, yes. A Nebraska seventh-grader was kicked out of school for showing up with a pair of blunt-edged safety scissors. In Kansas a thirteen-year-old was suspended for racial harassment after he sketched a Confederate flag on a piece of paper. At an elementary school in Gimli, Manitoba, kids can be turfed out for hugging.

The numbnuts faculty of the school calls that "inappropriate touching."

Score one for our side though—after long and thorough soul searching the city council of Birmingham—England's second largest city—has decided that the nursery rhyme "Baa Baa Black Sheep"…is not racist.

Perhaps it was the black mother who stood up at a city council debate and pointed out, "The rhyme is about black sheep, not black people."

I wonder how you say "Duh!" in Birminghamese?

One is tempted to laugh at all this Pecksniffian stupidity. One would be wrong.

Zach Jones thought it would be a good laugh to write a column in his student newspaper on a subject that affects every human being and over which many people—children and adults—spend an inordinate amount of time chuckling: flatulence.

Maybe Zach's column wasn't Pulitzer Prize material, but it was a long way from *Mein Kampf*—although you wouldn't know it from the way authorities reacted. The high school principal took all twelve hundred copies of the student newspaper containing the column and *locked them in a safe*. Zach was relieved of his column. The teacher who helped Zach was fired. The district school superintendent thundered onto the battlefield, declaring the column to be "obscene."

"If that column's obscene, then I deserve the death penalty for some of the things I've written about," commented an observer. An observer by the name of Dave Barry, who just happens to have won the Pulitzer Prize for humour. He shakes his head about the silliness, but he's not surprised. "There are always going to be people in positions of power who don't have a sense of humour," he says.

Okay, no sense of humour. But how about two brain cells to rub together?

YOU SHORT? NO PROBLEM A-TALL

Well, I see that short guys are getting shafted again. Funny. Thanks to the current epidemic of political correctness it is an offence just this side of plane hijacking to make mock of anyone's race, nationality, sexual orientation, political affiliation or religion.

But short guys? Hey. Sock 'em with your best shot.

A few years ago the songwriter Randy Newman had a smash hit with an acidic little ditty entitled "Short People" (basic message: short people are insignificant).

There's an Elmore Leonard novel called *Get Shorty* which got turned into a Hollywood movie of the same name. The Shorty of the title was played by Danny DeVito.

Who is... guess what? Knee high to a fire hydrant.

Bad enough that short guys get the diminutive end of the stick in the humour department—now scientists are wading in with evidence that short guys get shortchanged in the romance department too. A study conducted by a team of Polish and British researchers has concluded that tall men are sexually more attractive and have more children than short guys.

"Absolute nonsense," declares John Hemphill, a menswear salesman in Toronto. "I've done all right for myself. In fact I'd like to think short men have more sex appeal than tall men do."

Of course he would. Mr. Hemphill is five foot two.

"Total BS," declares Scott Matalon. He claims all a guy needs is a resonant, confident voice to charm the ladies. "You have to keep talking and talking to get women's attention. We make up for our height (or lack of it) with our personalities."

Mr. Matalon is five foot three.

Hey—as a guy who was five foot two until he was sixteen, I am not sneering, believe me. I grew up wincing under nicknames like Shortstuff and Shrimp.

I don't know why I took shortness as an insult. Napoleon was five foot six. Nikita Kruschev was five-three. Queen Victoria? Empress of an Empire on which the Sun Never Set? Five feet even.

John Keats? One of the greatest poets in the English language? Didn't even hit the five-foot mark.

Alas, facts seldom get in the way of a stereotype. A few years back an American shrink wrote a book called *Too Small, Too Tall*. It was an in-depth study of all the US presidential elections between 1904 and 1984, focussing specifically on the height of the candidates.

Conclusion: the taller candidate made it into the Oval Office more than eighty percent of the time.

Which is too bad. Think of some of the lanky boneheads that occupied that office.

Best short-guy putdown I ever heard? From the lips of David Lloyd George, British prime minister and statesman. Once, as an after-dinner speaker, he was introduced by an emcee this way: "I had expected to find Mr. Lloyd George a big man in every sense, but you see for yourselves that he is quite small in stature."

Lloyd George came to the lectern, pulled himself up to his full five foot one, looked down at his introducer and purred, "Where I come from, we measure a man from his chin up. You, evidently, measure from his chin down."

Short, tall—who cares? There's a famous old quote from Sophie Tucker that goes, "I've been rich and I've been poor—and rich is better."

Well, I've been short and I've been (relatively) tall—and I can tell you, it's attitude that matters, not altitude.

Sometimes I think that all the anti-short jokes are just jealousy. That fellow Scott Matalon that I mentioned earlier, five foot three?

His high school sweetheart was a six-foot model.

Loved to slow dance.

So did Scott.

Think about it.

DOWN ON THE FARM—THE GOOD OLD DAYS

It's ironic that the "Black spread" of my youth would qualify as a typical small farm. To a city boy like me it was as vast as Africa. A dizzying cavalcade of apple trees, pasture lands, wheat fields, still-water ponds and hardwood bush, not to mention groundhogs, red-tailed hawks, foxes and pheasants. And that was without even entering the menagerie that was the barn.

There a half-dozen dozy Holsteins chewed and lactated in the gloom. There were also pigs, a couple of draft horses and a gypsy band of barn cats. The barnyard was embroidered with a ubiquitous, shifting carpet of free-range chickens, forever breaking up and reassembling around the intrusion of people, dogs and the wheezy old John Deere. All of this was somehow crammed onto 150 acres of rock and clay on the outskirts of the small town of Fergus in southern Ontario.

I didn't grow up on that farm, but I grew out there a lot. As an adolescent nephew of Auntie Belle and cousin of her brood of ten, I had visiting rights and I exercised them enthusiastically.

I single out Auntie Belle not at the expense of Uncle Roy, who was the unquestioned patriarch of the place—regal, walnut brown and hickory thin from his years in the fields—but because when I saw him it was usually in the parlour or at the dinner table, and both those precincts were presided over by Auntie Belle.

Auntie Belle was large and warm and welcoming, just like the loaves of bread she baked in the wood stove—ten at a time, three times a week. She had twelve mouths to feed (not counting freeloading nephews) and most of what she fed them came off that farm.

Cider from the apples, syrup from the sugar bush, raspberries and currants from the canes and berry patches. Ham, bacon, chicken, turkey, beef, milk and cheese from the barn. Potatoes and greens from the vegetable garden out behind the summer kitchen. In late August they ate the corn they'd watched grow all summer. In spring they had the turnips which hadn't gone to market.

"Roosters and turnips pay the taxes," Uncle Roy used to say.

Did I mention they did all this without electricity? As newlyweds in 1923, the Blacks moved into a new log farmhouse, the walls all plastered and impervious to wiring. They never got to flip a switch until 1967, after all the kids were grown.

Grim and joyless? Hardly. During the great blackout of 1965 when the eastern seaboard power grid failed, plunging millions into darkness and chaos, it was just another day on the Black farm. They didn't even know about it. As usual that evening after supper they had a fire in the parlour. There was the low murmur of easy conversation and no doubt a fiddle tune or two from Uncle Roy and a couple of the boys.

I remember what it was like to sit in that parlour of a summer evening with the dusk coming on. The kerosene lamps transformed the room. Faces took on forgiving tones and glassware winked beguilingly. Sharp edges softened, harsh colours became muted. Folks farthest from the lamps were all but obscured; those closer to it glowed like saddle leather. You couldn't comfortably read fine print in that light, but you could absorb an awful lot of information just the same. Funny how with electric light, you see more but you get less.

They worked that farm for nearly half a century until Uncle Roy died. By then most of the kids had dispersed to pretty much every corner of Canada and Auntie Belle, having done the work of five farmhands for two generations, treated herself for perhaps the first time in her life. She travelled like Auntie Mame—Europe, Alaska, California, Nova Scotia and Newfoundland. She's gone now, too, but she left ten children and a still-growing gaggle of grandkids to remember her.

Folk singers, poets and editorial writers often write that small farms are dying, but they're wrong. To anyone who's ever known one, a small farm never dies.

JUST CALL ME UNSUITABLE

I had spent the whole of my savings... on a suit for the wedding—a remarkable piece of apparel with lapels that had been modelled on the tail fins of a 1957 Coupe de Ville and trousers so copiously flared that when I walked you couldn't see my legs move.
—Bill Bryson

Okay, men—the jig is up. Abandon your sweats and mothball your Levi's. Trot your sneakers and T-shirts down to the Salvation Army Thrift Shop for the delectation of society's more desperate and less discriminating dressers. For those of us who are *au courant* and in the know, comfort is out.

Men's suits are officially back in style. The style section of the *Globe and Mail* has given us a whole feature on how men will shortly be abandoning the casual look for the more traditional two- and three-piece outfits that ruled white-collar dress codes for most of the last century. Moreover, that journal of foppery *Gentleman's Quarterly* concurs. *GQ*'s style arbiters recommend a "minimum" wardrobe of three suits plus an ensemble of blazers, sports coats and assorted trousers to mix and match.

So there it is, guys. Nothing for it but to go out and surrender to the first clothier you see. Let him drape and encumber you with swatches of Hugo Boss and Armani while backroom gnomes jab straight pins into your wrists and ankles and rudely measure your inseam. Oh, yeah—and don't forget to pick up a half a dozen ties, too. Shouldn't set you back more than, say, a grand—maybe fifteen hundred bucks?

Excuse me while I laugh hysterically.

This menswear edict gets trumpeted from the ramparts every year about this time. The fashion fascists send out a spokesman to announce the death of "active sportswear," as it's called, and to herald the resurrection of the suit. And every year, a crushing majority of North American males blithely ignore the decree and go on wearing their polos and turtlenecks, Dockers and tennis shoes.

Every autumn some Style Stalinist tries to round us up and rein us in, like a schoolmarm with an unruly class. Fun's fun, they sniff, but the time has come to put away those dowdy duds, form up in orderly rows and dress like proper gentlemen.

Ain't gonna happen, folks. Oh, we'll each hang on to an emergency suit for weddings and funerals, and of course the boys on Bay Street won't abandon their capitalist monkey uniforms anytime soon, but for the rest of us, men's clothing options have just become too damned comfortable—especially compared to the suit.

The men's suit was always a profoundly stupid idea: too hot in summer, pathetically inadequate in the face of a Canadian winter and too bewildering all of the time. Are lapels wide or narrow this year? How many buttons per sleeve? Are vented jackets back in? How about flared trousers? To cuff or not to cuff? And where do you put your wallet, car keys, notepads and cellphone without making yourself look like a walking bag of walnuts?

For those who would argue that the business suit conveys a sense of authority and purpose, I have just two words: Jerry and Seinfeld.

It was Seinfeld who observed, "The suit is the universal business outfit for men. I don't know why people think it projects this image of power. 'We'd better do what this guy says, his pants match his jacket!'"

For me the concept of business-suit-as-Superman-cape was vaporized forever by a fellow named Chip Young, a freelance writer I knew many years ago in Toronto. Chip was known for three things: good writing, his silk-and-honey Tennessee twang and the fact that he never, ever wore a suit and tie. Not that he was a slob. Chip wore clean, pressed duds, but they leaned toward the sweaters and slacks end of the sartorial spectrum—which was unusual back then. Reporters and writers were expected to dress up for interviews or press conferences. I remember the time Chip showed up at the door of the premier's office in the Ontario legislature for a prearranged interview. Chip was wearing khakis, a polo shirt and a windbreaker. An officious minion from the premier's office stood in the doorway, looked him up and down with unconcealed disdain and asked him what he wanted.

"Ah'm heah to interview the Premiah," said Chip mildly.

"What?" huffed the minion. "Dressed like *that*?"

Chip smiled his lazy Tennessee smile and said, "Ah can affoad to dress like this. What's yoah excuse?"

WHEELBARROWS AND CHICKENS

There's a famous poem called "The Red Wheelbarrow" by William Carlos Williams. It goes:

So much depends
upon

a red wheel
barrow

glazed with rain
water

beside the white
chickens.

The poem is famous, I think, because in just sixteen words, it sums up the ineffable magic of the here and now. I like to think of Williams—he was a country doctor in New Jersey as well as a poet—walking across a farmyard one morning, black bag in hand, perhaps after assisting at a childbirth or sewing up some hired hand's cut leg, coming around the corner of a chicken coop, seeing the wheelbarrow and the chickens and being transfixed by the…perfection of it all.

It is a poet's gift—and task—to discover the magnificent in the mundane. For most of us it takes a bigger jolt than the sight of a wheelbarrow and a clutch of chickens to be reminded of the preciousness of each moment. But the world is still brimming with strange and miraculous happenings that ought to take our breath away if we're paying attention.

Consider the story of an unusual six-year-old boy named James Leininger of Lafayetteville, Louisiana. James loves airplanes—particularly World War II airplanes. Always has. Once when he was out shopping with his mother, he pointed at a toy airplane. His mother remembers, "I said to him, 'Look, it has a bomb on the bottom,' and he told me, 'That's not a bomb, it's a drop tank.' I had no idea what a drop tank was."

James Leininger did. He was two and a half years old at the time.

James's fascination with airplanes continued. He played with nothing but toy airplanes and even dreamed about them. Then the dreams became nightmares. "I'd wake him up and he'd be screaming," his mother recalled. "I'd ask him what he was dreaming about, and he'd say, 'Airplane crash on fire, little man can't get out.'"

Gradually, the little boy's memories became more specific. He "remembered" that he flew a plane called a Corsair. "They used to get flat tires all the time," he said. He "remembered" that his pilot name was also James. Once his mother asked him what happened to him in the Corsair. "Got shot," he said. Where? "Engine." Where did it crash? "Water." Who did it? "Japanese." How did he know? "The red sun on the plane."

One day his mother made meat loaf for dinner—something she hadn't made since before James was born. Little James looked at his plate and said, "Meat loaf! I haven't had this since I was on the *Natoma*."

Natoma? Neither parent had ever been involved in the military or aviation. The only aviation-related items in their house were James's toy planes. Where was the kid picking up this stuff? His father Bruce began to investigate. He searched the internet, combed through military records and discovered that during World War II a US aircraft carrier called the *Natoma Bay* was stationed in the South Pacific. Twenty-one of its crew died during the Battle of Iwo Jima, including a Corsair pilot named James Huston. On the afternoon of May 3, 1945, witnesses saw Huston's plane take a Japanese hit to the engine. It crashed into the sea and sank.

Young James doesn't have the nightmares anymore and his memories are fading as he grows older. But the story isn't fading, it's growing. Bruce Leininger contacted the families of the twenty-one crew members who died in the Battle of Iwo Jima. All of them spoke of "a spirit" visiting them in the years since the war.

And they all want to meet young James Leininger. This year, his parents plan to take him to the *Natoma Bay* veterans' reunion.

So is it a crock? I suppose it could be. Professor Paul Kurtz, a paranormal investigator at State University in New York thinks so. He says the parents are "self-deceived."

"They're fascinated by the mysterious and they've built up this fairy tale," he says.

Could be. And perhaps a red wheelbarrow is just a red wheelbarrow.

PART V:

PAINS AND PLEASURES

IN PRAISE OF DOING NOTHING

Lazybones, sleepin' in the sun,
How you 'spect to get your day's work done?
Never get your day's work done,
Sleepin' in the noon day sun...
—Johnny Mercer

Well, the dog days of summer are behind us, and that's a pity. It's the only time of year when hyperextended humans get to behave like...well, dogs. Just lying around, soaking up the rays, copping snoozes and scratching where it itches. The hot summer sun makes it hard to rush about the way we do the rest of the year, like Type A Chicken Littles. I love the dog days. They legitimize laziness and I am a certified lazy guy.

Which would make me an endangered species if scientists at the US National Institute of Mental Health had anything to say about it. They've been tinkering with monkey brains, trying to make them more, you know, productive. They've discovered that by suppressing a particular gene they can turn an ordinary, happy-go-lucky chimpanzee into an obsessive, goal-oriented worrywart who doesn't know how to relax.

"The monkeys become extreme workaholics," a researcher burbles, "as evidenced by a low rate of errors performing tasks, irrespective of how distant the reward might be."

In other words, they've managed to take a perfectly happy, well-adjusted animal and transform it into a neurotic working stiff. Great moments in science.

I'd be worried about the mental health institute boffins if I didn't happen to know that they are micturating into the wind. They haven't got a prayer of winning this war. There are just too many lazy folks like me out there.

And not just on this side of the pond. A recent Associated Press survey of ten European countries declared the laziest people in Europe to be...the Germans! According to the survey, Germans spend an average of just seven hours a day on paid work and housework combined. Mind you, Norwegians take more time off—about a hundred and seventy days per annum, which, if you do the math, works out to damn near half the calendar year. Sweden sounds like a sweet gig for a lazybones too. The Swedes have just introduced a program that will pay workers seventy percent of their salary for staying home for a year, enabling the jobless to "gain experience by taking their place." The only proviso: the stay-at-home worker cannot take a salaried position somewhere else.

Oh, heck.

Even as I write, there's a conference being held in a small Swiss village near the Italian border. It is called the National Convention of the Idle. The organizers promise a full afternoon will be devoted to a debate on the virtues of laziness. Well, correction—not a full afternoon. There will be a break from 1:00 p.m. to 3:00 p.m. for a mandatory siesta.

Perhaps delegates will take something to read in their hammocks. They can choose from one of two books on the international bestseller list that are veritable paeans to laziness. *How to Be Idle* is a passionate screed written by an indolent Brit name of Tom Hodgkinson.

Mr. Hodgkinson argues that, far from being a bad thing, idleness is our key to salvation. The economy, he says, should be geared to freeing us from labour, not harnessing us into sixty- and seventy-hour workweeks.

He wants us to "throttle back the vast overheated engine of our industry, curtail its exploitation of our natural resources, reduce its output of waste and pollution, and provide everyone with lives of increasing leisure."

Corinne Maier is even more radical. She's the French author of *Bonjour Paresse*, which translates as "hello, laziness." Mme Maier contends that it is every good citizen's duty to slack off at work. In a chapter daintily titled "Business Culture, My Arse," she says most corporations are cesspools of nepotism where people get ahead by who and not what they know, so why not "spread gangrene through the system from the inside?"

Not surprisingly, Mme Maier's book was not well-received by the state electric utility she works for. The company has threatened her with disciplinary action and summoned her to a hearing to discuss her "bad working habits."

Regrettably her moment of truth has been postponed several times because the necessary personnel haven't been on hand to conduct the hearing.

It's all those staff vacations. The average French worker works about three hundred hours less each year than the average North American.

Sounds like Mme Maier's compatriots don't really need to read *Bonjour Paresse*.

ACCUSTOMED AS I AM

Guess which single activity scares more people than anything else in the world. More than falling off a mountain or being lost in the jungle or getting stuck in an elevator with Sheila Copps, even.

Making a speech. Specifically, standing up on one's hind legs in front of a roomful of strangers and putting one's mouth in gear.

It's an odd phobia when you think about it. You're not treading water in a tank full of hungry hammerheads. Nobody's waving a blowtorch over your nether regions. What's the worst thing that can happen when you get up to make a speech? You start to hiccup? You discover your fly is open?

Actually it can be much, much worse than that. As a guest speaker, I've been standing up and mouthing off to rooms full of strangers for the past twenty-five years. I've speechified to doctors in Toronto, lawyers in Vancouver, building contractors in Florida and Canadian soldiers in Germany—not to mention sanitation workers in Sudbury and prospectors in Flin Flon, Manitoba. I've heard the words "Ladies and gentlemen, please welcome, Arthur Black..." hundreds and hundreds of times.

And yes, I still get butterflies in the belly before I speak.

But mine is not the irrational fear of the toastmastering tenderfoot.

I come by my nervousness honestly. After all, I was once guest speaker at a convention of Canadian meat packers.

They are a robust confederacy, your meat packers. Indeed, an occupation that consists of poleaxing large animals, dismembering them and rendering their body parts into shrink-wrapped gobbets on Styrofoam trays is unlikely to engender a brotherhood of effete and hypersensitive aesthetes. These particular meat packers were rowdy, rude and profanely huge, with thighs like wharf pilings and forearms like beer kegs.

And those were the wives.

What's more, they had been golfing all afternoon, fortifying their performance on the links with lusty belts of rum and flagons of beer dispensed, I was informed, from a golf cart specifically designated as a travelling saloon.

They were, in short, drunk. And the open bar at the back of the convention hall suggested that they wouldn't get sober any time soon.

It is never a good idea to give a speech to a roomful of drunks. But it's a profoundly bad idea to give a speech to a roomful of drunks who have been genuinely entertained by a speaker just before you.

In this case I was preceded by a stand-up comic who was—I swear I'm not making this up—stone blind. Not only blind, but paralyzingly funny. This guy gingerly tap-tapped his way up to the microphone with his white cane—and then he laid them in the aisles. The audience loved him. He was very, very funny.

Then it was my turn. "HERE'S ANOTHER GUY GONNA MAKE YEZ LAUGH!" thundered the emcee, grabbing me by the sleeve and hurling me toward the microphone.

I didn't. Perhaps they'd squandered their entire empathy quotient on the blind comedian or maybe I was overpoweringly mediocre that night, but they didn't laugh. Not once. They drank, they mumbled, they looked at their watches and yawned and scratched, but they did not laugh.

My speeches normally run about forty-five minutes. My speech to the Canadian meat packers went on for seven and a half years, it felt like. Near the end I was sweating and shouting hoarsely to be heard—I think they were very close to rushing the stage and beating me up—then, like a bad dream, all the noise in the room stopped for one moment. No one coughed, no one scraped a chair and, for a nanosecond, I stopped reading. Total silence.

And into that silence floated the voice of a woman in the audience—not loud, but perfectly audible to everyone in the room. And what she kind of…murmured…into that moment of crystalline silence was:

"Why doncha shaddap and siddown, ya asshole?"

Yes, I thought to myself. Why don't I? And I did.

It was easily the worst night I've ever spent on a stage, but it was also perversely liberating. I had crossed a horror threshold. After the meat packers, no audience has held much terror for me.

But making a speech is never a complete cakewalk, nor should it be. Tension drives all things vital, be they violin strings, vocal chords—or that electric void between a speaker and his audience. One day you, dear reader, will be called upon to bridge the gap between a lectern and some strangers in a darkened hall, armed only with your tongue and your wits. Here are some tips that will make your ordeal easier.

Use technology. Print out your notes in at least sixteen-point type, bold faced and double-spaced. Nothing's more daunting than glancing down at a page of pithy observations only to see what appear to be randomly scattered carapaces of tiny insects.

Avoid alcohol. Okay, one small glass of wine, but that's it. Any more and you run the risk of coming off too loud, too slurred and too dumb.

Pack heat. Always keep at least one all-purpose zinger in your quiver to defang hecklers. When one drunk kept interrupting comedian Steve Martin, he paused, put on a bemused look and said, "Oh, yeah. I remember when I had my first beer…"

I've always been fond of the deceptively withering, "Thank you. We are all refreshed and challenged by your unique point of view."

Observe the three Bs: be audible, be brief and be seated. And the greatest of these is brevity. No audience ever complained that a speech was too short. The best advice I ever had about public speaking came from a laconic Finlander who asked me to "say a few words" to a roomful of Rotarians in Thunder Bay many years ago.

"But Einar," I hissed as he pulled me to the stage, "what should I speak about?"

Einar looked at me and muttered, "Speak about three minutes."

SCROLLED ANY GOOD BOOKS LATELY?

If you've had the dubious pleasure of fighting your way through any of Canada's larger airports lately, you may have noticed a brand new booth tucked in amongst the sunglasses, ball caps and T-shirt boutiques.

It's a service called Teleporter. For twenty bucks or so they'll let you rent a DVD player along with a copy of the movie of your choice. You take these on board, watch the movie during the flight, then turn the player and the movie back in at your destination airport.

There's an even cheaper piece of entertainment hardware that's been available at airports for years. It doesn't need batteries, cables, modems or disks. What's more you can jam it in your hip pocket, drop it, kick it, even spill coffee all over it and it still works like a charm.

They call it a paperback.

Remember how a few years ago some cybertech gurus were proclaiming the death of books? They assured us that it was only a matter of time before the only paperbacks or hardcovers around would be in museums and we'd all be reading—make that "scrolling"—the latest bestsellers on our laptops.

Well, sure. Who wants something cheap and portable like a pocketbook when you can give yourself carpal tunnel damage and a five-alarm migraine staring at the phosphorescent screen of a two-thousand-dollar temperamental piece of gadgetry that's fragile, needs a power source and is prone to crashing unexpectedly?

The success of electronic books has been highly underwhelming, while the death of the conventional book has been—to cop a line from Mark Twain—greatly exaggerated. As a matter of fact, the simple book is turning out to be more durable than anyone ever suspected.

A couple of decades ago, in the first flush of cyberphoria, the British Broadcasting Corporation grandly announced the inauguration of the Domesday Project. It was to be a computer-driven multimedia version of the famous, thousand-year-old Domesday Book.

The idea behind the project was to bring some pizzazz to the fusty old pages of the famous book and at the same time showcase Britain's growing electronic sophistication. Big thinkers were hired and computational brainiacs were charged with developing special computers to handle videodiscs of text, photographs, maps and archival footage.

That was back in 1986. Earlier this year, the Domesday Project was officially declared dead. Why? Because the technology used to create the project has been eclipsed. Everything developed for the project is already obsolete. Unreadable.

As opposed to the real, eleventh-century Domesday Book, which is in near-perfect condition and available to the reading public in the Public Record Office in London.

That's one thing the webheads didn't count on: incompatibility. As Katie Hafner wrote recently in the *New York Times*, "In an ideal world, all the information from an old machine would float effortlessly, invisibly, over to the new one with the click of a mouse. But the real world has other plans. New software is incompatible with the old. Ancient cables won't fit the latest machines."

Tell me about it, Katie. I've got a Commodore 64 in the closet that I plan to use very soon—just as soon as I can figure out how to weld it to an anchor chain.

As for books, I don't think they'll ever die. Mind you there's a good chance they'll be forgotten by a large chunk of the internet-infatuated public.

I am reminded of the story told by an instructor for an adult-education program at a community college not far from here.

One day a young student walked into the library area of the school and did a double take when he saw a wall of *Encyclopaedia Britannica* volumes in front of him.

"Whoa! What are all these books?" he asked incredulously.

Encyclopaedias, he was told.

"Awesome," he replied. "You mean somebody printed out the whole thing?"

CARS: TOO SMART FOR THEIR OWN GOOD

Had your car recalled yet? If not, don't feel left out. At the rate things are going—and providing you're behind the wheel of a vehicle of more recent vintage than a 1983 Westfalia—you should be getting a letter from your dealer sometime soon.

Consider: DaimlerChrysler is recalling 135,000 sedans to replace faulty seat bolts.

GM wants to have another look at a few thousand specimens of a dozen car and van models built since 1999 to fix the airbags, steering linkages and trunk releases.

Volkswagen is asking owners of Passats built between 1990 and 1997 to bring in their buggies for some work on defective front seat heaters.

There are also recall orders for Dodge Dakotas (headlights), Kawasakis (oil leaks), Honda minivans (leaky gas tanks), Mitsubishis (accelerator pedal problems), Chevrolet Silverados (unsealed windshields) and Toyotas (slippery floor mats).

And those, friends, are merely the recall notices that went out to the public in *one week* recently.

What's the problem here? Are car makers building lousier cars these days? No, they're just building cars that are way more complicated.

At the risk of sounding like a dinosaur, I have to say that I remember riding in the rumble seat (look it up, kiddies) of my brother-in-law Roy's Model T Ford. It had hand-operated windshield wipers, skinny rubber wheels with wooden spokes, and a brass horn mounted on the door frame that went AY-OOOOOOOO-GAH when you squeezed the rubber bulb.

And no worries about the electric starter malfunctioning. There wasn't one. You started the car by jamming a steel hand crank into a slot below the radiator, giving it a reef, then running back to the driver's seat before the car took off on its own.

Roy's Model T wasn't fast or smooth riding but it was reliable. Most cars were back then. After all, there wasn't that much that could go wrong. And when something did go wrong, you didn't have to be a diagnostic technician or a mechanical wizard to fix it. I also recall a '52 Pontiac my Dad drove that had a tendency to jam in first gear.

My Dad's solution? He'd get out, open the hood, smack the gear linkage with a ball-peen hammer, close the hood, get back in the driver's seat and drive on.

I try not to even open the hood of my car nowadays. What's the point? It looks like the command centre for the Pickering nuclear plant in there, with sleek, grey, anonymous modules ticking and humming away, all carrying stern admonitions.

Warning! Never open when hot.

Poison! Causes severe burns.

Danger! Exhaust gases present.

Caution! See manual.

And the mystifying Reminder: Use ATF Dexron as fluid fill.

Can you remember when Volkswagen Beetles came with a wooden yardstick you dipped into the gas tank to measure how much fuel you had left? I can. Seems impossibly neolithic when I read about the latest "automotive breakthrough"—something called iDrive.

iDrive is a knob that you'll find in the centre of the dashboard on the latest models of BMW. It can be moved in eight different directions and that gives you access to—get this—*seven hundred* different functions.

What kind of functions? Everything short of a moon landing. iDrive puts you in charge of communications (telephone), navigation (guidance, scroll-down road maps, GPS etc.), entertainment (radio, CD, DVD) and climate (heat, AC, air distribution).

But those are just the major groupings. Secondary menus include options like OB data (on-board computer and maintenance operation, don't you know) and settings (activation and deactivation of vehicle settings such as traction control).

All I can say is, Earth to BMW: I don't give a flying lug nut about all that crap—and it does not improve my highway confidence to think that the guy at the wheel of the oncoming BMW is bent over fiddling with his iDrive to check his latitude and longitude.

I don't want a dashboard console with seven hundred functions not counting the DVD/audio CD-R/MP3 player—I want a car that conforms to the philosophy of those early Model A and Model T Fords. Somebody once asked the man who created them, Henry Ford, what colours his cars came in. Ford fixed the inquirer with a flinty glare and grumped, "You can have any colour you want. As long as it's black."

That's all a car driver really needs. That, and a ball-peen hammer.

A CROSS TOO HEAVY TO BEAR

A long time ago, in another life, I was lucky enough one summer to take a gypsy trip right across Canada. Fetched up one day in a tiny town the name of which I don't remember, near the New Brunswick–Nova Scotia border. Acadian country. The French started pioneer colonies here back in the late fifteen hundreds. It's still very French. The day I passed through that unknown town was market day. The people were out in throngs. There were fiddlers and dancers. There were booths and stalls all along the main street, and townsfolk were offering jams, jellies, preserves, woodcarvings and folk-art doodads for the front yard.

And in one stall, quilts.

Including the most beautiful quilt I had ever laid eyes on. It was blinding white, with a single jet-black emblem repeated over and over. The quilt was meticulously stitched, impeccably finished...I had just one small problem with it. The black design that was repeated all over the quilt?

Swastikas. The crooked cross that Hitler and his thugs made world-famous. The beautiful quilt was covered with swastikas.

Needless to say, I didn't buy it. Some of my best friends, etc.—and anyway, who would want to be associated in any way with the single most repellent symbol of the twentieth century? Not me, thanks. And I had to wonder about what Nazoid thoughts might be percolating among the citizenry in that bucolic little burg.

Turns out I was overly paranoid, as usual. The Acadians knew, instinctively perhaps, that the swastika was a revered symbol thousands of years before the world ever heard of Nazis. Ancients in India drew swastikas to represent the trajectory of the sun across the sky. Over generations the swastika evolved into a kind of stylized solar wheel, an emblem of the sun's pureness and power of regeneration. Swastikas have appeared on Persian carpets, as garlands around the sacred Buddha—even on Greek and Cretan coins of antiquity.

Here in North America, Indians used dyes and pigments to trace swastikas onto petroglyphs. Near as anthropologists can figure, the New World swastika represented the four directions—the ones we call north, south, east and west.

There's even a gentile connection to the swastika. In the time of the Romans, underground Christians disguised their familiar cross as a swastika to avoid religious persecution.

Billy Graham and the swastika? Hard to picture.

Nevertheless, it can't be denied that the swastika has a long and honourable history as a symbol of peace and fruitfulness. It was the swastika's bad fortune (and ours) that, in the 1920s, the stark and simple design with a history of positive associations caught the eye of a demented paperhanger from Austria. Hitler appropriated the swastika, claiming it as an emblem of Aryan superiority.

Amazing what power a simple symbol can have. Away back in the early years of the twentieth century, gold seekers and hard rock miners settled in a small community in northern Ontario, near Kirkland Lake. They called it Swastika, and Swastika it was for the next forty years, until loathing for the Nazi dictator persuaded the town fathers to bury the name of their town and rechristen it with something more patriotic.

Thus, the town of Swastika renamed itself Winston, to honour Winston Churchill, the man whose image was about as far from Adolf Hitler as it was possible to get.

Here we are in a new millennium. The Beast of Berlin has been dead for better than half a century and yet his malevolent effect on a morsel of graphic art lives on. Aside from skinheads and bikers with low foreheads, the very sight of the swastika still inspires revulsion wherever it arises.

Pity. It's a fine emblem with (aside from one brief historical blotch) an honourable pedigree. I hope one day we can reclaim it and return it to its rightful significance. Of course it will take guts.

The kind of guts I wish I'd had when I had a chance to buy that Acadian quilt.

A FEW WORDS ABOUT FACIAL HAIR

There are several thousand valid reasons to loathe and despise Osama bin Hidin' and his verminous pack of psychopathic lunatics. I would like to add one more.

They've given beards a bad name.

Beards are not only common among the mujahedeen, they're mandatory—ordained by a warped interpretation of the Koran which also sentences women to spend their lives living under blankets.

But even without the recent bad press, it's been a long time since beards have had a really good public image. It wasn't always that way. Canada was once decidedly beard-friendly. Our first prime minister, Sir John A. Macdonald, flirted with facial fuzz from time to time. George Brown, his political rival and founder of what became the *Globe and Mail*, sported a hedge of chin whiskers that could have been used to sweep chimneys. Back then, a good full beard denoted prosperity, steadfastness and... well, virility. Most public figures, if they wore trousers, also wore beards.

Times change. Check out the White House in Washington or Whitehall in London—scarcely a five-o'clock shadow, never mind a chin whisker. Same on Parliament Hill. There's nary an unshaven mug in Cabinet (as befits a collection of submissive human sock puppets). Matter of fact,

I can't think of any major Canadian public figure who's bearded. Even Don Cherry shaved off that goofy goatee he sported for a while.

There is a serious dearth of positive bearded role models out there. Nowadays beards flourish only in environments friendly to Middle Eastern fundamentalists, obscure university profs, Grateful Deadheads, lumberjacks, mountain men and religious zealots with private gun arsenals and multiple wives.

Plus...well, me, actually.

Aside from a rash (pun intended) moment in the late seventies when I allowed my jaw to be clear-cut in order to raise money for charity, I've had an upholstered chin for more than thirty years.

Why? Why not?

The question isn't why some men have beards, but rather why most men voluntarily submit to the barbaric custom of scraping the bottom half of their faces with a sharp instrument seven days a week and sometimes twice on Sunday.

The Irish playwright and intellectual George Bernard Shaw, who had enough fur on his face to knit a throw rug, said his beard was inspired by his father.

"I was about five at the time," said Shaw, "and I was standing at my father's knee whilst he was shaving. I said to him 'Daddy, why do you shave?' He looked at me in silence for a full minute, before throwing the razor out the window, saying, 'Why the hell do I?' He never shaved again."

Still, there's no denying that some folks just can't handle the sight of a fur-rimmed mandible. I sense it, sometimes, when I'm introduced to a stranger and they recoil like they've been asked to do a slow dance with Fidel Castro. Some folks just flat out don't like beards.

But that's okay. I've found that, by and large, I don't much like people who don't like beards, so my face fur serves as a social marker buoy to help us avoid close contact.

And anyway, I think the tide is turning on beardophobia. Tom Hanks showed the world that beardos can be good guys. In the movie *Castaway*, Hanks cultivated a crop of facial fleece that cried out for a Massey–Harris combine harvester. (Mind, you he was marooned on a desert island. His only option would have been self-mutilation with a clamshell.)

Yet it's not as if we're entirely bereft of other positive bearded icons. We have it on biblical authority that Jesus and his disciples wore beards. For every Marx, there's a Moses. For every Ted Kaczynski, there's a Kenny Rogers.

Not to mention the most famous bearded hug-bunny of all—the guy who'll be making house calls near the end of December.

PS: If you're going to leave a treat, make it ginger ale, not Coke or Pepsi.

Colas can leave an unseemly stain on white whiskers.

THIS WON'T HURT A BIT

All this fuss about sleeping together. For physical pleasure I'd sooner go to my dentist any day
—Evelyn Waugh

I'm not a vengeful man, but I wouldn't mind running into Dr. Goldfarb in a dark alley some evening—preferably with a pair of heavy-duty Vise-Grips in my mitt.

Goldfarb was my dentist back when I was a kid. Correction: he was my yanker. "Extractionist" is the term I believe he used. Dr. Goldfarb did not straighten, brace, bridge, drill or fill his customers' teeth, he just pulled them out.

It was a dentally unenlightened era to say the least, and I came from a relatively large family living on a relatively small weekly paycheque. Hence there was no mollycoddling of cavities. Got a toothache? We know how to deal with that, my lad. Plenty more where that one came from (well, a couple of dozen, anyway). Open wide. Hold on. There. Keep that wadding in your mouth until the bleeding stops. Next.

Dr. Goldfarb had the forearms of a longshoreman and the compassion of a Nazi. He instilled in me a mortal fear of reclining chairs, white coats and anyone operating metal paraphernalia anywhere close to my mouth. For a time I couldn't even bear the thought of my own dinner fork touching (what was left of) my teeth.

And for about twenty years, I never arrived for a dental appointment without being snookered to the eyeballs with valium, painkillers or at least three and possibly six fingers of Crown Royal. I'm okay with dentists now. I go to my appointments un-self-medicated and clear of eye. Dentists don't scare me anymore.

But it's not me that's changed; dentistry has. Consider a Montreal-based business called Galerie Dental—Canada's first combination dental clinic and...art gallery.

Galerie Dental is the brainchild of two Montrealers, Jean Fortin and Marc Raper. M. Raper is a dental surgeon; M. Fortin, a general dentist. They've banded together to take the terror out of dentistry. Accordingly, you'll find no hard-backed chairs circling a coffeetable piled with furry-paged, twelve-year-old copies of *Maclean's* and *Reader's Digest* in the Galerie Dental waiting room. Instead there are comfy couches and plump armchairs. For diversion there are glossy art books scattered about and canvases by Quebec artists hanging on the walls. Soft classical music oozes from the sound system. For the more culturally downscaled, there's a flat-screen TV showing movies (but not *Marathon Man*). M. Fortin says the idea was to offer "a peaceful feeling not like a dentist office, not institutional."

Why the artwork on the walls? "It gives you another reason to go to the dentist," says one patient. "You get there early to look at the art. It's a very, very peaceful place."

And for die-hard dentophobes, a relaxing treat awaits even after their chair time is up—a massage administered by a registered masseuse who also works out of the gallery.

Classical music...art exhibits...a massage...Dr. Goldfarb, are you listening?

And then there's HealOzone.

This device is a German invention only now showing up in select dental clinics across Canada. You know that part of the dental duet where the dentist cranks you back in the chair, fixes that Cyclopean high beam full in your face and fires up that drill that sounds like a falsetto chain saw?

Well, forget it. With HealOzone you get a soft silicone cap snugged over your affected tooth, then a few painless squirts of ozone gas pumped into it. The gas kills cavity-causing bacteria after which the tooth is remineralized naturally. Proponents claim that with HealOzone a dentist does seventy-five percent less drilling. Small cavities require no anaesthetic at all.

Does it cost more? Hey, do bears use Delsey? *Of course* it costs more. But money has never been the issue with dental work. Pain avoidance is the point. Take my wallet, wife and first-born, Doc, just don't hurt me.

Of course there's an inexpensive way to handle the dental experience. My pal Carmen has no problem with her dentist. When she sits in the dentist chair she simply relaxes, waits 'til he tells her to open wide and just as the dental probe is about to enter her buccal cavity, she reaches her right hand down, grasps the dentist in what (in other circumstances) would be considered an extremely intimate embrace, and murmurs, "Now we're not going to hurt each other, are we?"

Wish I'd thought of that with Dr. Goldfarb.

A LOAF OF *PANE*, A JUG OF *VINO BIANCO* AND THOU

A reporter from the *Vancouver Sun* called me up last week and asked me to name my favourite vacation. It was a simple question that I'd never really thought about before, and given that I've driven, flown, sailed and hitchhiked over a fair chunk of the planet, it's a poser you'd think I'd have to ponder for a bit.

Instead I blurted out "Tuscany" almost before the reporter had finished the question.

Tuscany. Specifically a town called Lucca. Very specifically, a centuries-old farmhouse-villa deep in the rolling olive groves about a ten-minute drive from Lucca.

We stayed there with some friends about five years ago and I've never forgotten it. Don't think I ever will.

If you like the bar scene in Whistler, the nightlife in Cancun or the electric thrill of the Vegas strip, chances are you'd hate Tuscany. It's everything those places are not. A columnist for the Milan daily *Corriere della Sera* put it better than I can. Cesare Fiumi wrote, "It's not that we're rich. In fact Italians earn less than just about anyone else in the European Union. Even Icelanders make more money than we do. But we know what to do with the little we have. Our ideal is to live in a little village surrounded by vineyards, where church bells ring every hour, the wine is made locally, and vegetables grow in the back garden."

If that sounds like an Italian version of some corny old Jimmy Stewart movie—well, so be it. The fact is, for two weeks that's pretty much how we lived—sprinkled with excursions to other Tuscan towns like Pisa, Siena, San Gimignano and the living urban art museum that is Florence.

Even Lucca, the closest town, is a marvel. It is surrounded by a massive red-brick wall that was built when Columbus was still alive and Canada was a place to get codfish, beaver pelts and not much else.

And I mean massive. The top of the wall is wide enough to land a plane on, with groves of full-grown oak trees, bicycles for rent and hundreds of strollers and cyclists at all hours of the day and night.

The best thing about the wall around Lucca is: it keeps the cars out. Only police, emergency and some delivery vehicles are permitted within the walls, which means pedestrians rule the streets, just the way they did before the internal, infernal combustion engine came along.

And that, as Martha would say, is a good thing. Because if Tuscany is the golden apple of Italy, cars and trucks are the worms in its core. Vehicle traffic in Tuscany—in all of Italy, actually—is ghastly and terrifying. There is no observed speed limit, pedestrian tourists are all but classified as designated game animals and every Italian driver feels it's his or her sacred duty to pass any vehicle going in the same direction.

It's not that Italians are bad drivers—I suspect that they're more skilful than North Americans. They have to be just to survive. The concept of the Sunday drive never caught on in Italy. Every vehicular excursion is a replay of the chariot race scene in *Ben Hur*.

So how does a pedestrian get around? Well, it helps if you're deeply religious, because just crossing a street in Italy is an act of faith. You can spot the North American tourists easily—they're plastered against the wall, peering uneasily at the river of careening metal in front of them, vainly waiting for low tide. Italian pedestrians have no such qualms. They just step into the street chatting airily, blithely ignoring their impending deaths. "You've got to act as if you have a right to walk in the street," an Italian explained to me. Sure enough, the cars and trucks slow down at the last possible moment and the pedestrian is allowed to cross.

But all of that happens on the other side of the wall when you're nibbling at the *piatto del giorno* at a café in Lucca—or when you're sitting on the porch of a certain farmhouse-villa just a few minutes away, sipping a goblet of the local Chianti while dusk paints the hills and fields in purple, sienna and umber, and the fireflies emerge to arabesque through the olive groves.

It's not exhilarating like a black-diamond run at Aspen. It's not swanky like the nightlife in New York and it lacks the jittery mainline energy of a blackjack table in Vegas. A country vacation in Tuscany offers none of those thrills.

And that's the whole point.

THE SIMPSONS? FIFTEEN? *AY, CARAMBA!*

I remember the first time I beheld a Matt Groening cartoon. It was back in the late seventies, in an issue of *Rolling Stone* magazine. Groening was the (at the time) unknown artist behind a cartoon strip called *Life in Hell*, featuring two amateurishly drawn rabbits exchanging very clever *bon mots*.

"Funny guy—too bad he can't draw," I remember thinking.

Huh. Matt Groening is the guy who later invented *The Simpsons*.

So what do I know?

That memory came swimming back at me a while back as I read a newspaper story pointing out that *The Simpsons* series contract had just been renewed through to the 2010 season and that it was currently in its fifteenth season. Think about that. *The Simpsons* has been on TV for fifteen years.

Fifteen years? That's the age of a decent single malt Scotch, for heaven's sake! Is it possible that we've been watching the adventures of dumdum Homer, übercoiffed Marge, kid genius Lisa and demon-spawn Bart for that long?

Afraid so. And in that fifteen years we have seen celebrities the likes of Elizabeth Taylor, Johnny Carson, Ringo Starr and some two hundred other household names line up to have their voices—and often their

Groeningized caricatures—inserted in one episode or another of *The Simpsons*.

The thing that sets *The Simpsons* apart from other TV comedy series is that after fifteen years—it's still funny. *Happy Days* isn't. Reruns of *M.A.S.H.* seem annoyingly chatty. *Cheers* is a tedious bore, and the humour in *All in the Family* feels positively geriatric.

And the current competition? Get real. Shows like *Friends* and *Frasier* can share the deep end of the pool with *The Simpsons*, but so-called comedy series like *Will and Grace*, *Suddenly Susan* and *Third Rock From the Sun* deserve to be relegated to...well, say the fourth rock from the sun, minimum.

Robert Thompson, who runs the Center for the Study of Popular Television at Syracuse University, rates *The Simpsons* as not only world-class, but an all-time classic.

"Mentioning *The Simpsons* right next to Mark Twain does not bother me at all," he says. "There are more funny things in a single act of a single episode of *The Simpsons* that there was in the entire run of *Suddenly Susan.*"

Amen. Of course, enthusiasm for the ongoing adventures of the Simpson family is not universal. The show has its detractors. Religious fundamentalists routinely excoriate *The Simpsons* for its unflattering portrayal of "family values." Right-wing nutbars see it as a threat to the Amurrikin way of life. And Dan Quayle (Ned Flanders incarnate) was briefly famous for going on TV to condemn Homer, Bart and most of the mythical town of Springfield for everything they collectively stood for.

The rest of the planet does not agree. *The Simpsons* is a cultural icon and a television staple in no less than seventy countries around the world.

I am not a TV fan. Fred Allen called it "chewing gum for the eyes" and I agree. But *The Simpsons*? For me that show redeems everything vile about the medium. And Dan Quayle? If you're reading this...

Eat my shorts.

WHAT WERE THEY THINKING?

Only two things are infinite—the universe and human stupidity. And I'm not sure about the former.
—Albert Einstein

We come now to one of my favourite human categories: Dumb Moves, or What Were They Thinking? What, for instance, was that twenty-eight-year-old woman from Houston, Texas, thinking as she tootled along in her cherry red SUV near Blaine, Washington, last month?

Well, actually we know what she was thinking. She thought she was on her way to Vancouver, Washington. She was half right. She was headed for Vancouver, for sure, but the other one. Vancouver, BC, four hundred kilometres to the north. Our intrepid voyageur steadfastly ignores all telltale clues such as signs reading "This Way to the Mounties," "Large Snow-Covered Foreign Country Ahead" and "Last Chance to Change Greenbacks Into Funny Money." She pulls up to the Canada Customs booth and smiles serenely at the attendant.

Ignoring, no doubt, her order of an Egg McMuffin with fries, the Canada Customs agent asks her to pull over to a search bay for a security check. That's where officials open her glove compartment and find...

A live hand grenade. The border crossing at Blaine, Washington, goes into total, full-terror-alert lockdown for one hour.

Now we don't know that the woman actually placed the hand grenade in the glove compartment, but somebody—her husband?

A trick or treater? John Ashcroft?—did.

And my question is: what were they thinking?

What, for that matter, was Dale Robin Hersh of Franklin Lakes, New Jersey, thinking when he arrived at Sao Paolo airport on an international flight from the States recently? When he was told that new Brazilian customs procedures required him to be fingerprinted and photographed—just as all Brazilian citizens must be when entering the US—Mr. Hersh snarled, said some bad words, glowered at the camera and held up his identification card for the photographer.

As well as his middle finger, conspicuously extended.

If Mr. Hersh had been a mob *capo*, a Hell's Angel or a defenceman for the New Jersey Devils, one might understand his Cro-Magnon intemperance. But Mr. Hersh is a pilot with American Airlines. He knows the airport drill better than most. And he not only knowingly committed a jailable offence—he provided photographic evidence of the commission of the crime.

What was he thinking?

As it turned out, he didn't do jail time, but he did have to fork over a US $12,750 fine for showing contempt to authorities. Still feeling witty, Mr. Hersh?

Speaking of rigid digits—you know those impossibly dumb spam ads you get on your computer screen from time to time offering penis enlargement pills—the ads that *nobody* could ever *possibly* be *stupid* enough to fall for? Well, *Wired* magazine did a little survey and found one online penis pill purveyor who had taken orders from six...*thousand* customers. They paid an average of a hundred dollars for two small bottles of bogus tablets. Only works for Pinocchio, guys...

And since we're down in the nether regions, I'd like to offer a special What Were They Thinking Commemorative Plaque to the folks at the College of Physicians and Surgeons of BC. A urologist with the college was quoted in my morning paper recently as to how doctors are "re-examining issues surrounding the procedure of circumcision."

Seems the medical community is considering the radical hypothesis that circumcising baby boys might...hurt.

"I did circumcisions as an intern—the kid screamed for a bit, you put a soother in his mouth and that was it," the doctor said. But that was forty years ago, when parents were routinely told that infants couldn't feel pain. Now, the urologist says, he feels terrible. "We know that circumcision is far from painless for the infant. The evidence is now overwhelming that circumcision is extremely painful."

Hmm. A razor-sharp scalpel sawing away at the unanaesthetized genitals of a newborn infant…

Painful, you say? Astounding.

Why did you think the infants screamed, doctor?

What were you thinking?

FOOD FOR THOUGHT

Slow down, you move too fast.

The old folky duo Simon and Garfunkel sang that refrain in a song they recorded back in the early sixties.

We failed to take their advice. Today, nearly four decades later, our cars go faster, our airplanes go faster—hell, even our bicycles go faster.

And of course, our food goes faster than ever.

Who, in the 1960s would ever have dreamed that one day we'd be lining up to buy such things as IncrEdibles or McDonald's McSalad Shaker? IncrEdibles is actually a whole line of fast foods, but the show-stopper product is...well, it's macaroni and cheese on a stick. It comes in a cardboard tube. Just pop it in the microwave for sixty seconds, peel off the cardboard and eat it like a Popsicle. The McSalad Shaker is designed to save food preparers from the exhausting and debilitating practice of actually having to go through the gruelling process of tossing a salad by hand.

No need with this baby. McSalad Shaker comes in a plastic cup, complete with a rounded top. Just pour on the salad dressing, cover the cup, give it a brisk flick or two of the wrist and hey—dinner is served. A McDonald's press release points out helpfully that McSalad Shaker "fits neatly into your car cupholder."

Like I want to meet a guy who's driving toward me on the highway with a cellphone in one hand and a salad fork in the other.

The movement toward ever-faster fast food is nowhere more rampant than on the shelves of you local bookstore. Martha Stewart has a book out called *Quick Cook*. You will also find such titles as *New Food Fast*, *Life's on Fire: Cooking for the Rushed* and *Nice Timing: Gourmet Meals in Minutes*.

What's with the obsession for speed eating? John Stanton, professor of food marketing at St. Joseph's University in Philadelphia, says it's the inevitable price we pay for the hectic lives we lead.

"People want to eat the right things," says Stanton, "but when it comes to trading health for time, time wins."

Robert Berman agrees—enthusiastically. He's the guy who invented mac 'n cheese on a stick. He says, "People are constantly pressed for time these days. When I was growing up in the fifties, my mom made breakfast every day and the family sat down for dinner every night. It's a very different pace we live today. Breakfast is pretty much gone, as far as sitting down and eating. Lunch is on the way out, and dinner is under attack."

Maybe. But not for everybody. There's a counter-insurgency movement that started in Paris about fifteen years ago and is slowly, quietly making its way around the globe. It is called, oh, delicious irony of ironies, Slow Food. Delegates from fifteen nations (including Canada) signed the Slow Food Manifesto. Here is what they believe:

"We are enslaved by speed and have all succumbed to the same virus: Fast Life, which disrupts our habits and pervades the privacy of our homes.

Our defence begins at the table with Slow Food. Let us rediscover the flavours and savours and banish the degrading effects of Fast Food."

What can a panting, rat-racing also-ran say to that but, amen, brother.

And Beulah, peel me a grape. But slowly.

WE DIDN'T GET SICK

My travel writing career began with a call from the editor of Air Canada's in-flight magazine, En Route, *offering my partner and me a lavish, all-expenses-paid Caribbean vacation courtesy of the Bahamas Ministry of Tourism. All I had to do was write a nice magazine article about my trip. My travel writing career ended two weeks later with a call from the editor saying, "We can't run this." This is the travel story* En Route *declined to print:*

We didn't get sick. I'm stressing that right off the top, because nothing ruins a tropical holiday like a dose of Caribbean Quickstep or Tobago Trots. Nope, we didn't get sick, but I sensed we were in trouble when I caught myself humming the theme music from *Jaws*. Miami Airport can do that to you. Especially after your luggage arrives looking like it's been mangled by wolverines and a guy in a motorized cart gives you hell in Spanish and English—after *he*'s run over *your* foot. No matter, we're snowbirds desperate to catch our connector flight to the Bahamas. We arrive at the gate perspiring and gasping, three minutes before scheduled flight departure.

Keyword: scheduled. A half-hour passes. I ask when Flight 112 will be leaving. "Soon as I can find a pilot," the dispatcher drawls. Oh, yes, a pilot. Good idea. Eons later a pilot materializes and we are herded onto the tarmac toward what looks like a kayak with wings. We mortals will board this craft and defy gravity in a flight over shark-infested water not terribly far from the Bermuda Triangle.

The passengers include your correspondent, his increasingly thin-lipped Lifetime Companion, a covey of squally, overheated prepubescents and one Piltdown-sized, cigar-chomping bubba who looks like a hillbilly wrestler gone to seed. The kids are stowed in the back "just so's we can get off the ground," the pilot explains guilelessly. The rest of us winnow our way into the fuselage; the wrestler squeezing into the seat beside the pilot. The seat usually reserved for the copilot.

But it's a short flight, and the addition of a copilot would force one of us to make the trip lashed to a wheel strut. The plane waddles aloft and drones a hundred and fifty miles due east, fetching up at a landing strip on one of the smaller Bahamian cays. We eventually get to our hotel, scarcely five hours late.

"At last," I murmur to Lifetime Companion. "Let the pampering begin." I stride to the check-in desk, explain grandly that I am here to do a story about their fabled isle and I am ready to claim the luxury villa the Ministry of Tourism has reserved for me.

There is no reservation. They have never heard of me.

Perhaps it's Christian charity, or maybe it's the Bank of Montreal MasterCard and three pieces of identification I produce—whatever, they give us a room. It is not a swell room, but it beats the winged kayak. After three days of fruitless phoning I reach someone in the Tourism Ministry in Nassau. She knows about my assignment and is devastated to learn that the trip thus far has been a disaster. They will make up for it tomorrow when we fly to Nassau. There will be a lavish luncheon! We will be the guests of honour! We will have an escorted tour of the city! We will be put up in a splendid five-star villa! Reservations for dinner and a floor show have already been made!

The plane that is to pick us up is three hours late. We watch as it lands and blows a tire. We learn that there are no spare tires in stock. One will have to be flown in.

It is very hot in the unairconditioned terminal, and the cafeteria—by which I mean the Coke machine—is empty.

We arrive at our villa in Nassau hours too late for the luncheon and tour but in time, if we hurry, to honour our dinner reservations. Lifetime Companion softens, even hazards a grim smile. We might, I think to myself, pull this one out yet. She heads for the shower; I make for the villa office to find out what time they serve dinner.

The office looks deserted. I lean in the door, calling, "Anybody home?"

"COME IN!" screeches a fishwifey voice. Something that looks like a carpet slipper with teeth skitters across the floor toward me yapping and yipping.

"Ah, my name is Arthur Black and I jus..."

YAPYAPYAP

"COME IN! COME IN!"

"Ah, yes, ma'am, thank you. I ah...your dog..."

YIPYIPYIP

"COME IN! COME IN!" screeches the voice. *Why doesn't she come out?* The dog is shredding my pant cuff now. Dragging it along, I limp into the office and find...

A parrot. For five minutes I've been conversing with a blue-fronted Amazon.

I never find a human being or a restaurant, but we make do with two bags of peanuts and a couple of cans of lukewarm club soda lurking in the otherwise ransacked minibar. We no longer care about food or floor shows or...anything, really. Except getting the hell home.

Which we do, the next day. And for weeks we answer the obvious question from envious friends: "How was your trip?"

And we always say the same thing. We say, "Well, we didn't get sick..."

A WORM IN YOUR EAR

I have a disease. An inflammation. A virus. What's even worse, I'm about to pass it on to you. You will be infected by the following four-word paragraph scant moments after you read it. Ready?

"The Lion Sleeps Tonight."

Can you feel it yet? Is that eerie falsetto *weeheeheehee dee heeheehee-hee weeo weem* away already ricocheting through your cranium? Are the lyrics "In the jungle, the mighty jungle..." bobbing up in your subconscious like so many aural deadheads?

Sorry about that. I was suffering from STS, and according to Professor James Kellaris of the University of Cincinnati, the very best way to cure oneself of STS is to pass the malady on to someone else. And you're it.

STS? Stuck Tune Syndrome. The condition with which a piece of music—usually a *bad* piece of music—screws its way into your earhole and won't depart no matter what you do.

The Germans have a word for it—*ohrwurm*—literally, "earworm." The Portuguese are even more graphic. They call it *chiclete de ouvido*, which means "ear chewing gum."

Whatever you call it, it's a universal condition and a certified pain in the... ear.

Professor Kellaris reckons ninety-eight percent of us have suffered earworm infestations at one time or another.

Me? I've got an entire necropolis of the wriggly buggers bucking and writhing between my sideburns. Check this out:

Just one location: five-oh-nine on Danforth Avenue.
For the best used car buys in the town, try Ted Davy.
Ted Davy. Ted Davy.

Or how about:

Presswood bacon and Presswood ham,
Presswood bacon and Presswood ham,
Come, gather round children, and hear what I say,
Get Presswood ham from your grocers today.
There's wieners and sausages, bacon and ham,
Get Presswood ham just as quick as you can!

Those are radio jingles that I first heard when I was on hands and knees and wearing nappies more than half a century ago! They're still roiling around in my head today.

Professor Kellaris claims that most earworms disappear after an hour or two, but that's not my experience. I hate to think of the upper-story shelf space I've squandered by filling it up with worthless flotsam like "Brylcreem—a little dab'll do ya!" Not to mention "Winston tastes good like a (bap bap) cigarette should." And not just radio jingles. I may be the only person you know who can sing (sort of) "The Auctioneer." Including the chorus which goes:

Twenty-five dollar biddle now a thirty dollar thirty widdle ya gimme thirty make it thirty biddle 'em all a thirty dollar, who'dla bid a thirty now, who'dla bid a thirdy dollar bill? Thirdy dollar biddle now a thirty-five a widdle ya gimme thirty-five make it thirty-five biddle a thirty-five, who widdle a biddle that thirty-five dollar bid?

Can't remember where I left the car keys, but I'll take the lyrics of Leroy Van Dyke's ballad to my grave.

How to get rid of a really stubborn earworm? The professor recommends chopping wood, jogging up a mountain, getting an early start on your income tax return—anything that will distract and refocus your mind. He also suggests substituting another song for the one that's driving you batty—but that's playing with fire as far as I'm concerned. I tried substitution once when I couldn't get the song "Delilah" off my mind. What replacement tune could possibly be sufficiently hideous to cancel out Tom Jones ululating in my head?

Which is how I came to spend the next three days humming Paul Anka's "(You're) Having My Baby."

There is even a website for the earworm-infected. It's called *Maim That Tune*. Punch it up on your computer and it will play you a song even more execrable than the one that you're trying to download from your brain. And if the first song you hear isn't horrible enough, there's a button entitled "Try Another Tune, Sailor!"

Maim That Tune might work for some, but I still prefer the sadistic, personal approach—namely cornering someone and passing on the ear-worm directly. It doesn't have to be confrontational. This is a game you can play over the phone.

Here's my advice: the next time you're suffering from a musical brain cootie, think of some really annoying person. Phone them at a time you know they're not home and then hum, whistle or warble your deadly ditty directly into their answering machine.

And if you're thinking of slipping your serenade on to my answering machine, be forewarned.

It's programmed to answer your call with William Shatner singing "Lucy in the Sky With Diamonds."

IN PRAISE OF PRAISE

I can live for two months on a good compliment.
—Mark Twain

Pardon me for asking but...has anybody told you how great you look today?

I thought not. But don't think it's because you don't look good—you do. You look wonderful. It's just that not many of us—hell, hardly any of us—take the time or the trouble to spend a few words to acknowledge the obvious and simultaneously lift the spirits of the folks who cross our paths each day.

Oh, there are the toadies and BS artists who ladle out compliments like Pez pellets. I'm talking about the lickspittle brown-nosers so deftly skewered by Billy Crystal's sycophantic one-liner, "You look *faaabulous*!"

But that's not a compliment—that's baloney. (Not to be confused with Irish blarney. As someone once said, Baloney is flattery so thick we know it's not true. Blarney is flattery so thin we like it.)

You don't have to morph reality or make up fantasies to pay someone a compliment. What's so hard about telling somebody that you like the tie they're wearing or that they're looking trim or just that you're glad you happen to be sharing the same solar system? Doesn't cost anyone a cent and it just might turn somebody else's day around.

Ah, but it's just not in the Canadian character, is it? We're loners.

Introverts. We're the people who yelp, "Sorry!" when a stranger steps on *our* foot. Canucks don't come easily to the habit of shovelling out fulsome praise.

A pity. A pity we couldn't all be a bit more like...well, Ron Miller, for instance. Miller lives in Washington, DC, and for the past fifteen years he's made it his business to hang out on the street corners just...complimenting people as they stroll by.

He'll smile at a harried businessman and say, "Those are beautiful shoes you've got on there." Or he'll catch the eye of some browbeaten, deadline-dodging young subsecretary and say, "Ma'am, your hair looks just lovely this evening."

But this is Washington, DC—crime-ridden, junkie-infested hotbed of sleazy lobbyists, tinhorn politicians and paranoid G-men. Doesn't Miller get stonewalled, punched out or at least run in for public harassment?

Not on your life, he doesn't. The people in his neighbourhood love the guy. They call him the Compliment Man. The most common reaction he gets, is "Thanks. You made my day!"

As a matter of fact, Washingtonians didn't know just how much they needed Ron Miller until he up and disappeared one day. Vanished. That was when everybody who loved the Compliment Man suddenly realized that, hey, we don't know where this guy lives, if he's got a job or a family—we don't even know his name.

One newspaper ran a feature headlined "Where's the Compliment Man?" Radio stations picked up the story, and a Washington TV reporter did a man-on-the-streeter asking locals just how much they missed their daily dose of praise.

Fittingly, the story had a happy ending. Turned out Ron Miller hadn't been kidnapped, hit by a semi or whacked and tossed in a dumpster. He had just headed down to Florida on a whim to stay with relatives. But he missed his old Washington acquaintances as much as they missed him, and after two weeks he moved back north.

"When I got back, it was chaos," says Miller. They all said 'Compliment Man, you abandoned us!' but I didn't. I just took a little break." Miller is back on his usual beat, saying nice things to people and making them nicer in the process.

Who knows? Ron Miller is such a pro he could probably have coaxed a smile onto the blue-black jowls of Washington's greatest grump, Richard Milhous Nixon.

But maybe not. Nixon and compliments were a kind of natural oxymoron. There's a story about the time Nixon returned to his cabin at Camp David and announced, "I scored 126."

Henry Kissinger, never one to miss a butt-kissing opportunity, purred, "Congratulations, Mr. President! Your golf game is improving."

Nixon glowered at his Secretary of State and snapped, "I was bowling!"

Did I mention how great you look today?

PART VI:
PROMISES, PROMISES

HOW TO BE A RICH AND FAMOUS WRITER

Writing is easy; all you do is sit staring at a blank sheet of paper until the drops of blood form on your forehead.
—Gene Fowler

I am just a few years away from certified senior citizenhood and my Lifetime Achievement List still has a lot of blank spots. I have not (yet) learned to:

- wolf whistle
- play boogie-woogie piano
- tie a reliable clove hitch
- fix anything remotely mechanical

Actually, my "to do" list is a lot longer than that, but space is limited, so let me concentrate on what I have managed to accomplish.

I have written books. Eleven of them, as a matter of fact. Pretty paltry compared to walking word factories like Pierre Berton and Stephen King—but still…eleven books. Not too shabby. It follows that I must be rich, right?

Har followed by har. This is Canada, chum, where a runaway bestseller is anything that sells five thousand copies. The author's standard share of the list price? Ten percent. Average price of a book: twenty bucks. Even writing a bestseller leaves you with just enough money for a down payment on a second-hand beater.

Am I bitter? Hell, no. Why should I be bitter?

A mite jealous, maybe, when I pick up a copy of the *New York Times*, turn to their bestseller list and see that a book called *Star: A Novel* is sitting in thirteenth place, just behind Stephen King's latest opus.

Star: A Novel is the work of an ex-compatriot of mine—and yours—Ms. Pamela Anderson. You remember Pammie. She's the blonde bombshell from Ladysmith, BC, who parlayed a daunting set of gravity-defying jugs into a Hollywood career. Pam became the star of *Baywatch*, a show about lifeguards on a beach. Pam's acting, which consisted pretty much of jiggling in skimpy swim togs while standing on said beach, led to a couple of movies, a lot of magazine centrefolds, and now this: a novel.

Star: A Novel is about a celebrity who, wait for it now, starts out as a small-town girl with big boobs and becomes a sensation on a TV show called... *Lifeguards, Inc.*

Not terrifically original, for sure, but Pam is new at this, remember. And it's not as if she starved in a garret to write the book. As a matter of fact, she restricted her authorial input to one day a week (Fridays, including a catered lunch) for a mere seven months.

James Joyce took seventeen years to write *Finnegan's Wake* and eight to write *Ulysses*. Pam turned out her bestseller in twenty-eight days. Impressive, considering Pam's... um, lack of literary apprenticeship. As she told a reporter for the *Washington Post*, this whole book-writing business can be darn confusing.

"Like, chapters," she complained. "How many pages are in a chapter? How many chapters in a book? I needed some guidance."

And she got it. The truth is, Pam didn't actually, you know, "write" her book. She had twenty-eight lunches with a guy named Eric Shaw Quinn. Mr. Quinn, a professional Hollywood hack, passed the guacamole with one hand and scribbled notes with the other.

So Ms. Anderson didn't so much write her book as "chat" about it—but no matter. Pam is on the *New York Times* bestseller list and the coast to coast book tour and "The Letterman Show" and "Entertainment Tonight." And I'm wondering if it's too late to learn how to play boogie-woogie piano.

Could be worse. I could be like Henry, who suffered the ultimate indignity for writers. Not only did his book *A Week on the Concord and Merrimack Rivers* tank with readers and critics (1,000 printed, 294 sold), his publishers told him they were throwing out the unsold copies because they were taking up valuable space in the warehouse. Henry asked that they be sent to him. When they arrived and were safely stowed in Henry's house he wrote this melancholy entry in his diary: "I now have a library of nearly nine hundred volumes, over seven hundred of which I wrote myself."

Henry—did I mention that his last name was Thoreau?—was just a hard-luck kind of guy, I guess. Unloved by critics. Ignored by readers.

And born about a century and a half too early for silicone implants.

DRUGZ

There's a grand documentary by islander Mort Ransen about logging on Salt Spring Island. It's called *Ah... The Money, the Money, the Money*. That title went ricocheting through my head following the horrendous Mountie murders in Mayerthorpe, Alberta not so long ago. You may recall that RCMP chief Anthony Zaccardelli and Deputy Prime Minister Anne McLellan wasted little time finding the nearest news microphones to declare that the tragic incident just showed the inherent dangers of marijuana grow ops.

Well, they were right and they should know. They helped to make them that way. Grow ops are potentially dangerous places because marijuana is illegal and hence expensive. It's expensive because, for at least the last half century, we have ladled out hundreds of millions of law enforcement dollars for policemen, undercover agents, drug busts, drug snitches and undercover stings not to mention courts and judges and jail time—all in an attempt to stomp out the marijuana business.

How have we done? Here's how we've done. When I was sixteen, I knew exactly two people in the world who smoked marijuana—a Montreal jazz player who was my landlord and his girlfriend. Forty-five years of assiduous and enthusiastic law enforcement later, I see kids smoking pot in a downtown park in the middle of the day. I smell it on the wind half a dozen times a day.

I asked a visitor from Ontario—a newcomer to the island—how long he figured it would take him to score some dope on Salt Spring. He laughed. "About five minutes," he said.

I think marijuana's here to stay, folks.

The irony is—we've been here before. For thirteen years, between 1920 and 1933. That's when the world's biggest illegal drug market—the USA—declared Prohibition, outlawing the manufacture and importation of alcohol. Did Americans stop drinking? No, they just paid a lot more and risked going to jail to do it.

The Prohibition equivalent of our BC Bud was bathtub gin and rotgut rye. What did happen is thugs and crooks like Al Capone and Dutch Schultz grew sleek and fat on illegal booze profits. A lot of Canadians with fast boats did very well for themselves too.

Something about dealing with public addictions brings out the Keystone Kops in us. There's an old expression about closing the barn door after the horses have bolted. Our drug policy is not so much closing the barn door. It's more like placing the poultry under arrest.

Did you hear about the big bust on Galiano Island recently? Oh, yeah. This woman had this little "operation" going in her restaurant there. Every week the same ten or twelve people would mysteriously show up, same day, same time...go inside for two maybe three hours...and then mysteriously melt away into the Galiano greenery.

Something fishy going on for sure.

But our G-men were all over it. Victoria HQ sent in a four-man undercover team. They checked into a five-star B & B and put out the story that they were interested in picking up some island real estate. Nobody thought too much about it—even though the guys seemed to spend most of their time drinking coffee in the restaurant.

But then they sprang their well-oiled trap. Walked up to the cash register, flashed their ID and informed restaurant owner Deb McKecknie she was busted. The charge: running an illegal gambling establishment. To wit: a granny bingo. Did she make a lot of money from this front? Not a dime. She just gave senior citizens a place to play bingo once a week. Nobody made any money. The players just recirculated the dough among themselves.

Solicitor General Rich Coleman was having none of that. "The law is the law," he intoned with great originality. Gotta keep a tight rein on gambling, you know. Well, Mr. Coleman would know all about that too. He is part of the government that has doubled the number of slot machines in British Columbia since it's been in office. The return from officially sanctioned gambling puts $850 million into government coffers each year.

So in the end, it doesn't really matter if you're Al Capone or Elliot Ness. A grow op or a government. Your motivation is the same. The money, the money, the money.

FAME IS THE NAME OF THE GAME

In the future, everyone will be famous for fifteen minutes.
—Andy Warhol

Fred Allen once described a celebrity as "a person who works hard all his life to become well-known, then wears dark glasses to avoid being recognized." Fame's a curious commodity, to be sure. A little surprise package that can turtle-wax your glide path through life or burn your fingers to the bone. Elvis and Jimi and Janis all had their fifteen minutes on the world stage, but came to ends as squalid as any skid row junkie's. That's the Catch-22 of fame: you're never exactly sure when your fifteen minutes are up.

Take Vaughan Meader. There was a time, about forty years ago, when he was the second most famous man in all of the United States. The most famous American at the time was John F. Kennedy. Vaughan Meader was a household name because he could do a devastating impression of JFK. He was a sensation at nightclubs from Los Angeles to New York. He put out a comedy album called *The First Family* that became the fastest-selling record in history. Vaughan Meader was well on his way to becoming even more famous, but then on November 22, 1963, three rifle shots rang out during a presidential motorcade through Dallas and instantly, nobody wanted to hear anybody making even gentle fun of John Fitzgerald Kennedy.

Meader tried shifting gears. He put out an album without his trademark Kennedy impersonations. It sank without a ripple. He tried singing and stand-up comedy in smaller bars and nightclubs. Audiences yawned and trickled out the exits. He lived the American dream in reverse, going from riches to rags.

Vaughan Meader went from hero to zero in one day. His fifteen minutes were up.

In time, Meader became a chronic alcoholic, then a crack addict. He's still alive, but not by much. He's lost all his teeth and is in the late stages of emphysema. Incredibly, he still dreams of fame. "I'd like to come out with something, just one song, and be a hit. To hear my words and music on the radio, to me, would be a bigger thrill than anything."

And then there's Charles Webb. He wasn't quite as personally famous as Vaughan Meader, but his work was. Webb wrote a novel called *The Graduate*, which was turned into the classic movie of the same name starring Anne Bancroft and Dustin Hoffman. In 1967 Charles Webb was the toast of Broadway and Los Angeles, as rich and famous as Vaughan Meader's wildest dreams. Publishers were at Webb's door waving open cheque books. Hollywood was his for the asking.

And Webb turned it down. All of it. He formally forfeited all claims to *The Graduate* and gave away the fortune he'd received for the movie rights. He and his wife turned their backs on two homes they owned. They took to living in their van. They even sold off their wedding presents.

They moved to England, where they've lived ever since, getting by doing menial jobs—short-order cooking, dishwashing, fruit picking—even janitors in a nudist colony.

And why? Were they nuts? On drugs? Nope, they just had a problem with fame. "The success felt phony," Webb said. "It wasn't slumming for slumming's sake. It was the need to study something—to understand something. And being short of money was part of it. There's nothing wrong with wealth. It just didn't work for us."

Fame is a demanding mistress. Some people, like Elvis, Jimi, Janis and Vaughan Meader get gobbled right up by it. Others like Charles Webb have to throw it right out of the house to survive.

And a few—a very few—handle it with class. Like the poet W.H. Auden. When he was young and on the way up, someone asked Auden what effect he thought fame might have on him, should he ever be so anointed. Auden reflected for a while and then said, "I believe that I would always wear my carpet slippers."

And he did. Which is why when he later became Britain's most renowned poet, it was commonplace to see Auden at a fancy dress ball or a black-tie dinner, resplendent in tails, bow tie and cummerbund, with a pair of very ordinary carpet slippers on his feet.

Now that's how you handle fame.

SEEMED LIKE A GREAT IDEA AT THE TIME

I don't ask much from life. I don't expect the stretch limos, flotillas of groupies or thousand-dollar bills to light my Cohiba panatellas. I have no interest in becoming Lord Black of the Millpond, a guest on the *Tonight Show* or of winning that Lottery for Life—a red velvet bunk in the Canadian Senate.

No, I only have one unrequited desire: to have, in my lifetime, one great idea.

Is that so much to ask? Archimedes got his revelation in a bathtub. Newton got his under an apple tree. Einstein brainstormed $E=MC^2$ at his blackboard, and we can guess where Thomas Crapper was sitting when he got his inspiration to invent the flush toilet.

One great idea. That's all I ask for. I'm not trying to be a Thomas Edison, filing a thousand patents for everything from phonographs to light bulbs. I just want one.

I thought I had it back in grade seven. I remember almost nodding off at my desk while the teacher droned on about the rebellion of 1837. "Upper Canada was a tiny colony," he was saying, "not like the country of fifteen million (hey, it was a long time ago) that we live in today."

And I fell to doodling at my desk. Fifteen million...let's see...that would be fifteen...followed by six zeros. Imagine if I could persuade every Canadian to mail me...one penny.

That would put fifteen million pennies in my piggy bank. Or put another way, I'd have $150,000! Which was a fortune, back when I was a kid.

And that was as close as I ever got to a great idea. The Achilles heel that fatally hobbled my breakthrough concept was the fact that I couldn't think of a compelling argument to convince my fellow citizens to start mailing their pennies to me. My bombshell brainwave died aborning.

I admit, it sounds kinda lame a half-century later, but great ideas don't have to be blockbusters. Somebody invented the safety pin. Others came up with the zipper and the paper clip. Small items, but great ideas all the same.

And it's not like it's hard to get a patent even for a lame idea. Paul Hanson of St. Paul, Minnesota, just obtained a US patent for his all-new method of treating heart-related chest pain.

Hanson's solution: just drink limeade—but from concentrate. That's it—Hanson's great idea in a nutshell. He says it worked for him and the US Patent and Trademark Office was sufficiently impressed. Impressed enough to grant Hanson patent #6,457,474.

I think Michael Nelson's idea had a more obvious aura of greatness about it. Nelson recently opened a law office in suburban Orlando, Florida, leased himself a company car (Mercedes), printed up some toney-looking letterhead stationery listing all his law partners and began soliciting business from the families of convicted drug traffickers.

Did very well, too until a radio station investigated and found out that Nelson's law partners didn't exist and Nelson was not a lawyer. As a matter of fact Nelson was himself a felon, serving time for bank fraud. He could only "practise" during the day as he had to return to a halfway house each night. As near as investigators could figure, Nelson made "several hundred thousand dollars" before he was nabbed. Not surprisingly, Nelson's halfway house privileges have been revoked.

Still, great ideas don't have to be crooked and they don't have to involve lawyers (but I repeat myself). Take Dennis Hope of Gardnerville, Nevada. For the past twenty-three years, Mr. Hope has operated a real estate company, selling lots to interested customers.

But not in Nevada. Not even in North America. Not even on this planet. Mr. Hope sells land on the moon. Business has been so good that he's expanding. He'll now sell you choice lots on Mars and Venus as well. Going price: twenty dollars an acre.

How good is business? Very. Hope reckons he makes about US $270,000 a year.

And it's legal. It's based on something Mr. Hope learned in school as a kid. Back when I was doodling through my history lesson, Dennis Hope was paying attention. He heard his teacher say that, while the Outer Space Treaty of 1967 prohibits nations from owning celestial bodies, *it doesn't say anything about individual ownership*.

Hope says, "I even wrote to the United Nations explaining my plan and asking if they had a problem with it. Nobody ever wrote back."

But that was twenty-three years and $6.5 million ago. Great idea, Mr. Hope.

DOWN BUT NOT NECESSARILY OUT

Curious thing about panhandlers: the more there are, the more invisible they become. A couple of decades ago the sight of a man, a woman or a kid and his dog squatting on the sidewalks of our big cities would have been a reason to call the cops. Take a walk through downtown Vancouver, Toronto or Montreal these days and you can count on seeing at least a dozen panhandlers.

Except chances are you won't really see them at all. As the homeless among us proliferated, we non-panhandlers quickly became quite adept at looking right through these indigents on our sidewalks. We've learned to ignore them. Our eyes slide right by them as if they aren't there.

That's a dangerous condition. Why, a man like Gordon Elwood could die without even being noticed.

Which is pretty much what happened. I mean, you didn't hear about his passing, right? Not surprising. Mr. Elwood was never on *Letterman*. He wasn't a rock star or a pro hockey player. Gordon Elwood lived his seventy-nine years in relative obscurity, in a ramshackle bungalow on the outskirts of Medford, Oregon. He wasn't an unfriendly man, but he was just a mite reclusive.

And Lord, was he cheap.

He ate at soup kitchens as often as he could and made a point of buying milk that was past its best-before date. He got it at a discount that way. His clothes came from the Sally Ann and local thrift shops and he resented even that financial outlay. He kept his pants up with a bungee cord so he wouldn't have to waste money on a belt or suspenders. For spending money he collected bottles and cans and turned them in for the deposit. Each night he curled up in a greasy sleeping bag on a bunged-out sofa in his almost furniture-free house.

The odd thing was, Gordon Elwood didn't have to live that way. He was no hopeless hobo. He owned his own house, such as it was, and paid his bills, such as they were, from the proceeds of his TV repair work. Forty-six years ago Mr. Elwood took a correspondence course and taught himself to be a television repairman. For nearly half a century he fixed other people's TVs.

Didn't own one himself of course. You kidding? All that electricity?

Gordon Elwood never spent a dime on anything he considered frivolous. He even kept his house unheated. As a matter of fact, that's probably what took him out. After one particularly cold snap last winter, they found him huddled in his sleeping bag, stiff as a board. Pneumonia. The town of Medford put him in a pauper's grave and you would think that would be the end of Gordon Elwood's brief and miserable passage through life.

But it wasn't, quite.

Suddenly, an organization called the Gordon Elwood Foundation surfaced. It consisted of a board of directors—a couple of lawyers, an accountant, and other assorted business types.

Their job? To dispose of Gordon Elwood's estate.

All $10 million worth.

It turned out that Gordon Elwood was not only not poor—he was a closet stock-market dabbler. Pretty good one too—made himself a multi-millionaire.

And contrary to his public persona he was an astoundingly generous man. His whole estate is being liquidated in the form of grants, donations and pledges to various Oregon agencies that Elwood used while he was making his fortune—the YMCA, the Salvation Army, the Red Cross and a couple of non-profit organizations that help out people in need.

Interesting, though. You or I could have walked down a street in

Medford, Oregon, last summer, say, and passed an old geezer in second-hand clothes wearing a bungee cord for a belt and pulling on a carton of stale milk. Chances are he wouldn't even have registered on our consciousness.

Which would have been a pity. It's not every day you get a chance to meet a multi-millionaire.

I HEAR MUSIC

We must remember, Mozart and Beethoven didn't hear all the sounds we hear. They never heard the sound of a motor car starting, running, grinding, stopping. They never heard a telephone ring, or an airplane roar.
—Gregor Piatigorsky

And, one might add that, since he died in 1976, Mr. Piatigorsky (no mean tunesmith himself) never got to hear the telltale blip of a cellphone, the supersonic howl of an SST, or Eminem singing "The Real Slim Shady."

Strange critter, music, when you think about it. My dictionary defines it as "the art of combining vocal and/or instrumental sounds to produce beauty of form, harmony and expression of emotion."

That's a tad wordy. I prefer Debussy's take: he called music "the arithmetic of sound."

However you define it, humankind has been making music of one kind or another ever since some nameless Neanderthal used a pair of mastodon ribs and the floor of his cave to produce the world's first drum solo.

But why do we make music? Because it makes us feel better, I guess. Although that doesn't do much to explain musical aberrations like Muzak, Lawrence Welk—or Eminem singing "The Real Slim Shady."

Still, there's no accounting for musical taste. One person's Bach is another person's Britney Spears—even your mutt will tell you that.

No kidding. Researchers at The Queen's University in Belfast, Northern Ireland, recently put fifty dogs of assorted pedigrees into a room and played a whole bunch of music at them to see how they reacted.

The dogs were treated to all manner of music. Everything from Bob Marley to Vivaldi, from Beethoven to Metallica. Not to mention the aforementioned Johann Sebastian and Britney. Results? The scientists found that the dogs—be they Doberman or dachshund, Shih Tzu or St. Bernard—preferred classical music to rock and roll. They became calm and placid when Bach or Beethoven was piped into their room. When Metallica came on they went nuts, barking, howling and even snarling and biting at each other.

Hey—just like the audience at your average Metallica concert.

No question that the making of music has been transformed down through the ages. We've gone from mastodon bones to Moog synthesizers. From hollow logs to Hammond organs. And we've gone even further than that.

Consider: it is possible for me to go home this afternoon, flick on my computer…

And become an instant musician. Despite the fact that I can't finger a decent G chord on a guitar or get anything but a squeak out of a trumpet, my computer allows me to gain instant access to every sound ever made by any musical instrument ever recorded. All I have to do is pull down a program called Fruitloops. There I can choose from any number of drum styles incorporating my choice of tempo and beat. I can sound like Gene Krupa or Buddy Guy. I can then toss in a saxophone, electric guitar, bass, cello, trumpet, piano—you name it. It's all in the program. What's more, I don't have to learn how to fret a chord, handle a drumstick, or find middle C on the piano. There is no piano. All there is is my computer mouse.

Is this music? Well, I have my doubts. The scary thing is, if I do it well enough, you wouldn't be able to tell it from real music—the kind produced by actual musicians.

Is it the way of the future? I hope not, but I did notice a small newspaper item in the *Wall Street Journal* recently. Apparently the Pentagon has just purchased a carload of what they are pleased to call "technologically enhanced" bugles.

From now on, any member of a US funeral honour guard will be able to put one of these bugles to his lips, press a button, and emit a digitally recorded, technically perfect rendition of "Taps."

"It provides a dignified visual," explained a Pentagon official, "something families tell us they want."

Well, I suppose. But it ain't exactly a lone piper silhouetted against the North Sea playing "Amazing Grace," is it?

NEVER ON SUNDAY

Well, I see Nova Scotians came down—narrowly—against Sunday shopping. In a recent plebiscite, fifty-five percent of the citizens who voted said "No!" to the option of being allowed to fill a shopping cart, crawl the malls or bring home a two-four of Moosehead on Sunday.

This makes Nova Scotia the only province in Canada to retain that cultural fossil of yesteryear, the six-day shopping week. It also made Nova Scotians the butt of much smirking and derision in newspaper stories and business reports on television and radio across the country. Our ever-vigilant neighbours to the south noticed as well. To many Americans it must have been just one more pathetic example of Canoehead Frostbacks stubbornly clinging to their quaint and antiquated nineteenth-century quasi-feudal lifestyle.

"Nova Scotia voters reject Yankee materialism," simpered the newspaper *USA Today*.

Most Halifax retailers, who were (not surprisingly) in favour of open Sundays, went nuts when the voting results were announced. "We've just kicked a twenty-five million dollar boost to the economy in the face," grumbled one store owner. "A victory for the Amen corner," sneered another.

I'm sure if those wee-hours yukmeisters Ralph Benmergui and Mike Bullard (remember them?) were still around, they would be chortling hugely into the late-night ether about those bumptious Bluenosers and their backward ways. Imagine! Actually choosing to deprive yourself of a basic human right the rest of North Americans take for granted!

Well I say: good for Nova Scotia. They may be the last remaining people on this continent who have not been shucked and jived into believing that shopping twenty-four-seven is what life is all about and nothing is real unless you can buy it at the mall.

Just a reactionary old fart ranting? Well, maybe. It's true that I'm antique enough to remember when Sundays in Canada were truly a day of rest. There were no baseball games to line up for or movies to go to. You couldn't buy a beer or a book of stamps. All stores were closed, and if you turned on your TV all you got was an Indian-head test pattern to watch.

Sounds boring, but a funny thing happened with those Sundays. We took advantage of them to do things we couldn't do on the other, more frenetic days of the week. We actually used to make long, lazy afternoon-length visits to people in their homes—even have them back to our place. As families, I mean. Singalongs around the family piano were not unheard of. Books got read and gardens got weeded. Peaceable chores got tended to. Mum darned and sewed. Dad tinkered away at his basement workbench, doing no large damage to various malfunctioning household items.

There was plenty of downtime too—an hour or so in the hammock if the weather allowed, otherwise a snooze on the chesterfield with only the hypnotic tick-tock of the mantel clock to lull you even deeper into sleep.

I remember old pastimes that don't seem to be around anymore. Whistling. Whittling. Drowsy games of crib and canasta around the kitchen table.

Well, who's got time for that nowadays? And who needs homegrown entertainment, really, when you've got a beeping cellphone on your belt, five hundred channels on the boob tube and an ever-boinking computer in the den reminding you that *You've got mail!*

Besides, it's not as if Nova Scotians have entirely consigned themselves to the Dark Ages. As Bill Harrison, president of the Hotel

Association of Nova Scotia puts it, "Nova Scotia is a place where you can't buy a shirt on Sunday, but you can sure lose your shirt."

That's right—Nova Scotia casinos will still be wide open for business on Sunday.

The Nova Scotia government, which gets a Mafia-esque rake-off from the casinos, knows that a principled stand on Sunday shopping is all very well.

But some things are sacred.

ADVERTISING: THE NOT-QUITE EXACT SCIENCE

Let us consider the phenomenon of advertising. Some folks call it the bane of communication in the twentieth century, but it's been around a lot longer than that. Elizabethan town criers hollering, "Oyez! Oyez!" in Hyde Park? Advertising. Lady Godiva riding bareback (and bare everything else) through the streets of Coventry? More advertising. When you think about it, advertising has been ever with us. Marshall McLuhan called it "the cave art of the twentieth century."

Like all art, some of it is good and some of it is awful. I, for instance, have decided I will never purchase so much as a footstool from U-NIT-ED FURNITURE WARE-HOUSE! because their television ads are so annoying.

At the other extreme is the classic TV ad for Volkswagen. You remember the one? It opened on a blizzard scene while a voice asked if we ever wondered how a snowplow driver gets to work. Then they show a humble VW Beetle in the middle of a field of snow. We hear it start, we see its headlights come on, we watch it crawl steadily, dependably across our television screen. End of ad.

That ad showed no actors, no celestial choirs, no endless highways, no special-effects bells and whistles—it was so simple it was even shot in black and white!

Ad people still speak reverentially of "the snowplow ad" nearly forty years after it first aired.

At the other end of the spectrum there is the Just For Feet television commercial which didn't even survive one year. Advertising people call that one the "ad from hell."

It all started with a prosperous but not terribly well-known shoe company called Just For Feet that sells running shoes. In an effort to make themselves famous, they blew their advertising budget, hired the best agency they could find and signed up for the most expensive advertising slot available. The ad agency was Saatchi and Saatchi. They assigned their most creative people to the Just For Feet account. They came up with an ad and showed it to the Just For Feet president. He hated it, but the ad guys told him to relax. It would work like a dream. It was the best thing the agency had ever done. You stick with shoes, they told him. We'll take care of the advertising.

Chances are you didn't see the Just For Feet ad. It didn't run long, but then it didn't have to. It was scheduled to run during one of the most coveted—and expensive—time slots there is—the third quarter of the Super Bowl, when something like 127 million people around the world would be glued to their TV sets. In a spot like that, the advertising agency has as much riding on a successful ad as the client does. Everybody wants it to be just perfect. Like—you know—that snowplow VW thing.

What went on the air was an ad that showed a squad of grim-looking white commandos riding through the desert in a military Humvee. They are tracking the footprints of a barefoot black runner. One of the bad guys drives ahead and offers the runner a cup of water laced with a knockout drug. The runner gulps it down, swoons and falls to the sand. While he's lying there, the bad guys gather round, force a pair of running shoes on his feet and disappear. We see the runner come to, look at his sneaker-shod feet and start screaming and shouting, "No! No!" In the last shot, we see him running hysterically across the sand trying to shake the shoes off his feet.

And this ad runs during the Super Bowl where more than a hundred million people can see it. As a writer for the magazine *Advertising Age* put it, "Have these people lost their minds?"

Instead of making the world feel warm and fuzzy about running shoes, the ad made people go ballistic. The *New York Times* called it "appallingly insensitive." The *Des Moines Register* suggested Just For Feet should change its name to Just For Racists. Other critics called the company neo-colonialist, condescending—even drug pushers.

What was supposed to be the greatest moment for Just For Feet became instead its greatest nightmare.

Their reputation was shot and so was their budget—the company had shelled out US $3 million to hire the agency, $1.7 million to purchase the time slot and another $2 million on newspaper ads urging readers not to miss the great Just For Feet commercial in the third quarter of the Super Bowl.

The ad from hell has cost Just For Feet nearly $7 million—not counting the lost customers.

And that Volkswagen ad I mentioned earlier? It cost Volkswagen exactly three thousand dollars—cheap even back in 1963 when it was made.

George Bernard Shaw once said, "It's just as unpleasant to get more than you bargained for as it is to get less."

I'm sure the folks at Just For Feet know exactly what he meant.

WHERE THERE'S A WILL

Made out your will yet? Didn't think so—me neither. Still, it's something to think about. You want to make sure you've done all the paperwork and looked after your family, your friends, your favourite charities and institutions.

And...oh, yes, your enemies.

They don't call it *last* will and testament for nothing. The piece of paper you leave behind is your very last chance to kick sand in the face of those who have plagued and perplexed you in this life. You and I are, of course, above such petty vengeance. But others have taken full advantage of the chance to taste the sweet sorbet of revenge from beyond the grave.

Such as? Well, such as Herman Oberweiss, a Texas farmer who passed away in 1934. But not before he informed his executors exactly how he wanted his estate to be disposed of:

"I don't want my brother Oscar to get a god dam thing I got," wrote Herman, "I want it that Hilda my sister she gets the north sixty akers...I bet she don't get that loafer husband of hers to brake twenty akers before next planting..."

Beyond-the-grave retribution goes back further than the dirty thirties. Away back in the seventeenth century, Phillip, the fifth Earl of

Pembroke, wittily and searingly took care of a couple of would-be inheritors:

"I give nothing to my Lord Saye, and I do make him this legacy willingly, knowing that he will faithfully distribute it unto the poor.

"I give to the Lieutenant-General Cromwell one of my words... which he must want, seeing that he hath never kept any of his own."

A century later another Englishman by the name of Edward Wortley Montagu ensured in his will that the British stiff upper lip maintained its keenly honed edge:

"To Sir Robert Walpole I leave my political opinions, never doubting he can well turn them into cash, who has always found such an excellent market in which to change his own.

"My cast-off habit of swearing oaths I give to Sir Leopold D., in consideration that no oaths have ever been able to bind him yet."

Some last-will-and-testamenters don't reserve their pot shots for individuals, they go for entire classes. Or even genders. Such as Mr. T.M. Zink, a full-time crank and world-class misogynist lawyer in Iowa who, on his deathbed in 1934, left an endowment to fund the Zink Womanless Library. Zink stipulated that each entrance would be flagged with a *No Women Allowed* sign, and that "no books, works of Art or decorations by women" would be permitted within the perimeter.

Lest anyone misunderstand, Zink explained, "My intense hatred of women is not of recent origin or development nor based upon any personal differences... but is the result of my experiences with women, observations of them and study of all literatures and philosophical works."

Be that as it may, Mr. Zink's will was overturned. There is no Zink Womanless Library and Mr. Zink is no doubt rotating in his grave.

Wearing, I like to think, pink lace underwear and a black garter belt.

Canadians too have indulged in revenge from beyond the grave. Witness the last will and testament of one William Dunlop, resident of southern Ontario back in the mid-nineteenth century:

"I leave my silver tankard to the eldest son of Old John, as the representative of the family. I would have left it to Old John himself, but he would melt it down and make temperance medals and that would be a sacrilege...

"I leave Parson Chavasse the snuff box I got from the Sarnia Militia, as a small token of gratitude for the service he has done my family in taking a sister that no man of taste would have taken."

I don't know a whole lot about William Dunlop, aside from his last will and testament, but based on that, I think I'd have been glad to stand him to a Kokanee lager to fill that silver tankard.

GOLD COMFORT

Well, I see by a report in the newspaper that it has finally happened. French and Italian metallurgists, the report says, have created high-grade gold in the laboratory for the first time ever! And they intend to start manufacturing the once-precious metal by the ton before the end of the year. Many experts believe, the newspaper reports breathlessly, that this unprecedented breakthrough will render gold jewellery, gold coins and all nations' gold reserves virtually worthless!

Or not. The newspaper in which the report appears is one of the trash tabloids you can pick up with your Oh Henry! bar at the supermarket checkout—which is to say, long on invention, short on fact. My hunch is the French and Italian metallurgists—if they even exist—are no closer to "creating" gold in a lab than were the gods of Greek mythology, the ancient Jews, the Egyptians, the Romans, the alchemists of the Middle Ages or the countless other dreamers and schemers who have tried down through the centuries to brew the precious metal out of base soup stock.

Humankind has been obsessed with gold for just about as long as humankind has been around. You can find goldsmithing details about the Ark of the Covenant in the Old Testament. One of our most enduring fables is about King Midas, the man with the golden touch. In their obscene lust for gold, Spain and Portugal conquered entire nations and tortured and enslaved tens of thousands of people. Here in Canada at the turn of the nineteenth century men left jobs, homes and families behind to hurl themselves against Yukon winters in a quest for Klondike gold.

And for what? For a metal that is pathetically soft, inherently fragile and amazingly scarce. All the gold ever found in the history of humankind amounts to about 125,000 tons, give or take a wedding band. As precious resources go, gold is pretty sad. Even if it was common as mud, there's not much you can do with it. Oh, you can make bracelets, cap teeth and coat electric wiring—but that seems a pretty piddly return for the centuries of devotion we've lavished on the stuff.

And even though most of the world has dumped gold as an official standard of value, we still suffer periodic bouts of gold fever. Just a few years ago the price of gold spiralled up to an incredible US $850 an ounce. True, it's now down around US $425 (as I type), but that's still pretty stratospheric for a so-called precious resource that you can neither eat nor drink, build a shed with, burn for fuel or put on your back for warmth.

So what is gold worth and who decides anyway? I don't know, but I'd bet a double gold sovereign that it's not a rational agency.

I'm pretty sure Andre Sharon would agree with me. He's a gold analyst on Wall Street who says, "If all men were rational, all politicians were honest and we had a world currency that was universally acceptable, then gold would drop to twenty dollars an ounce—and be overvalued at that."

Hmm. Rational men. Honest politicians. I guess we'll be on the gold standard for a while yet.

PART VII:
WACKO WEIRDNESS

THIS IS YOUR LUCKY DAY

You've got to ask yourself one question:
'Do I feel lucky?' Well, do ya, punk?

So spake Dirty Harry, an LA detective with severe attitude played by Clint Eastwood in the movie of the same name. The line was muttered while Harry was squinting down the cannonlike barrel of a .44 Magnum which was pointed at a tiny isthmus of pink flesh between the eyebrows of a certified bad guy. As it happened, the bad guy did feel lucky and went for his piece.

Turned out it was not his lucky day. But it got me to thinking about Dame Fortune, and the superstitious way most of us continue to genuflect before her (I think twice before walking under a ladder, don't you?). As a civilization we may be capable of putting people on the moon, but many folks still avoid black cats, tote lucky charms on their keychains and check their horoscopes before they go out the door.

Horseshoes are a good luck charm, though it's hard to figure why. Every nag in a horse race carries four of them. Only one horse ever wins.

But we continue to believe in luck—good and bad.

How about you—do you feel lucky? Or are you an Eeyore, convinced that fate has assigned you your personal black cloud that dogs you wherever you go?

Well, I've got good news—you can change your luck from bad to good and it doesn't involve four-leaf clovers, rabbit's feet or a St. Christopher medallion.

Richard Wiseman is a psychiatrist on staff at Hertfordshire University in England. Back in 1993 he decided it was time the phenomenon of "luck" was put under the microscope of science.

He advertised in several British newspapers, asking people who felt consistently lucky or unlucky to contact him and take part in a survey. More than four hundred people replied. Wiseman winnowed the group down to camps, one made up of people who felt blessed, the other of folks who thought life had dealt them a bad hand. Wiseman got them to keep diaries, fill out questionnaires and participate in experiments. In one experiment he got both "lucky" and "unlucky" people to look through copies of a dummied-up newspaper and count the number of photographs.

On average it took the people who called themselves unlucky about two minutes to complete the task. The people who considered themselves lucky were finished in mere seconds. Why? The second page of the newspaper contained a message that read, "Stop counting. There are 43 photographs in this newspaper." Almost all the "lucky" people spotted the notice. Almost none of the "unlucky" ones did.

Wiseman went further. Halfway through the newspaper he placed a large message in bold type that read, "Stop counting. Tell the experimenter you have read this and win 250 pounds sterling."

Again, the readers who called themselves unlucky missed the advertisement. They were too busy counting photos.

It was Wiseman's first concrete clue that good fortune is influenced by behaviour. Put simply, you can change your luck by changing the way you live. Here is what Wiseman concludes about "unlucky" people:

They are more tense than "lucky" people. And this anxiety tends to prevent them from noticing opportunities.

They live in a rut. They take the same route to and from work, shop in the same stores on the same day, talk to the same types of people at parties.

They perpetuate their bad fortune by an "everything happens to me" attitude.

Lucky people, on the other hand, are more loosey-goosey. They invite "chance" into their lives. Today they might take the bus to work; tomorrow they may ride their bike. They pick up hitchhikers. They talk to that flaky-looking woman by the chip dip.

And they're optimistic. They even see the bright side of bad luck by imagining how it could have been worse. Wiseman tells about one volunteer in his study who arrived for a session on crutches with his leg in a cast. He'd tumbled down a flight of stairs and broken his leg in two places. Wiseman asked him if he still felt lucky.

"Of course!" said the volunteer. "I could have broken my neck."

So there you have it. All you have to do to change your luck from bad to good is loosen up a little. Respect your hunches. Walk on the sunny side of the street. Take a few chances.

Unless you're facing a pissed-off guy holding a .44 Magnum.

THE CIRCLE GAME

I don't suppose I'll ever be interviewed by the *National Enquirer*. Too supernaturally deprived. I have never talked to an extraterrestrial, been kidnapped by aliens, or marvelled at strange and inexplicable spacecraft streaking across the sky.

But I have seen crop circles. In a farmer's field near Vanderhoof, a small town in the BC interior.

They were crop circles, all right. A good hundred feet in diameter. No sign of footprints, tire tracks or mechanical interference—just a series of circular depressions in which the wheat stalks had all been flattened in the same direction, as if by a giant steam iron.

What was it—a message from ET?

Not necessarily. Crop circles are a misnomer for the phenomena that appeared to paralyze Mel Gibson in the movie *Signs*. A better name would be crock circles.

They first gained public attention back in the 1960s, when farmers in the south of England began to notice strange areas of flattened grain in their fields. The fact that these fields were not far from the supposed ancient druidic site of Stonehenge jacked up the "Twilight Zone" factor right from the get-go. Before long the circles were appearing in grain fields in continental Europe, then in Japan, Canada and the US.

They all shared some common characteristics: the circles were big, of varying complexity, with no sign of human participation. And they always appeared overnight.

Theories were legion. Scientific types reckoned they were caused by rogue windstorms. Or maybe a plasma vortex of electronic force fields. Or perhaps geomagnetic currents from deep inside the earth were responsible. More mystical observers saw them as calling cards from aliens eager to communicate with earthlings.

Actually, what it was, was Doug and Dave.

Doug Bower and Dave Chorley, two good old boys who liked to knock back a few brews of an evening in a pub in Wiltshire, not far from Stonehenge. One Friday night back in 1978 after last call, Doug and Dave decided to have a bit of fun. They grabbed some rope and a few planks and headed out to a nearby farm. The next morning, a Wiltshire farmer was scratching his head and wondering what the hell had happened to his barley crop overnight.

For the next dozen years, Doug and Dave spent a couple of nights each week visiting farmers' fields under cover of darkness. They reckon that between 1978 and 1991 they created over a thousand crop circles in the Stonehenge area. A British newspaper reporter said, "Not so fast" and challenged the two to prove their story. They took the reporter out with them the following night. She watched as they tiptoed into a field between the plants and set up a pole with a string attached to the top. Then they grabbed the opposite end of the rope and began walking—Hey, presto!—a crop circle. Then they used the wooden planks to flatten the grain within the perimeter they'd created.

It looked good, but the reporter still wasn't convinced. The following day, she brought in one of Britain's top crop circle researchers and asked him whether he thought the creation was authentic. The expert's assessment? "No human being could have done this. These crops are laid down in these sensational patterns by an energy that remains unexplained and is of a high level of intelligence."

So are Doug and Dave responsible for the thousands of crop circles that have appeared from Valladolid to Vanderhoof? Of course not. But ninety percent of all reported crop circles in the world have appeared within fifty miles of Stonehenge. As for the ones Doug and Dave didn't do—the experts chalk them up to copycats.

Which experts? Carl Sagan, for one. The famous US astronomer (and tireless searcher for extraterrestrial life) concluded years ago that crop circles were an utter hoax. And the Committee for the Scientific Investigation of Claims of the Paranormal reports, "Approximately 100 percent of crop circles are man-made. We say approximately because we have to allow for dogs chasing their tales and other phenomena."

As for my Vanderhoof crop circles—they looked authentic to me, but I'm not an expert in the field. I do know a thing or two about human nature, though—and there was something a little "off" about the guy I talked to who reported the find. Nothing big—just a little sideways sashay of the eyeballs as he talked with a credulous gaggle of reporters about how "shocked and amazed" he was by his discovery.

He was saying all the right words, but he struck me as a guy with a great secret he couldn't wait to spill down at the local pub over a pint of beer.

Make that a crock of beer.

OF ALL THE CRUST!

Man does not live by bread alone.
—Eric Gill

Ah, yes. One of the hoariest clichés in the bromide Bible. But perhaps it's time for an update. Perhaps the new version should read, "Man does not live by bread at all." Or even, "Bread is dead."

You think I exaggerate? Consider this: Wonder Bread has filed for Chapter 11 bankruptcy in the United States. Wonder Bread! That pillar of American society that seemed as impregnable as Mom, apple pie and the right to carry concealed assault weapons!

Of course there are those who would argue that the manufacturers, Interstate Bakeries, should have been sued to death years ago for daring to slap a "bread" label on the spongiform confection they churn out, but that's a quibble for another time. The fact is, good old bread of all descriptions is under attack right now. Wonder Bread is merely the first casualty.

It's the low carb fad, naturally. Dr. Atkins and his calorie-cutting imitators have demonized what used to be known as the staff of life for its high carbohydrate content. And North Americans, obese and obedient little lemmings that we are, are waddling away from bread in droves.

Which, as ex-inmate #55170-054 Martha S. might say, is a good thing. On one level anyway. The fact that doughnut maker Krispy

Kreme recently suffered its first quarterly loss ever can only be good news for you, me and our cholesterol-clogged arteries. But this is not just about gooey doughnuts and plasticized white sliced bread. It is also about French baguettes and Jewish bagels. Russian black bread and German pumpernickel. Italian focaccia, Greek pita, Indian *naan*, English scones, Spanish *pan*—the list is endless. Just about every culture on the planet has a cake, a bread or a biscuit that anchors their identities and fills their bellies. We've been mixing salt, water and various flours together and shoving them into ovens for more that eight thousand years. *Aysh* is the Arabic word for bread. It also means life. This is pretty important stuff that Dr. Atkins and his Carbo Nazis are messing with.

Mind you, they're not the only ones tinkering with the goodies we put in our mouths. Russian scientists have just announced that they've figured out a brand new way to make chocolate biscuits—entirely out of blood.

Scientists at the Voronesh State Technological Academy began experimenting with blood recipes twelve years ago when they learned that a local meat processing plant was throwing out up to seven tons of animal blood every day. The filling of the biscuit they've come up with is made from cow's blood cells, and they claim it tastes just as good as the real thing. They also point out that blood contains virtually no fat and is loaded with iron and protein.

Dr. Atkins would be pleased. To say nothing of the International Vampire Guild.

Meanwhile, culinary breakthroughs from the US Army continue apace. You may recall that just a couple of years ago, American army chefs came up with a sandwich they said could stay fresh for up to *three years*. Yeah, I'm betting that would be a real taste treat after sitting at the bottom of some GI's backpack for thirty-six months.

But not content to rest on their laurels, these same culinary Columbuses have come up with dried food pouches that will last virtually forever. And when a soldier gets to feeling peckish, all he has to do is pull out a food pouch, rip it open and rehydrate the contents. By peeing on it.

That's right. No need to hump bulky canteens of water when you've got your own in-house irrigation system. Besides, you don't have to use your own urine. Swamp water will do, or a couple of scoops from any old mud puddle. There's a specially designed filter inside the dehydrated pouches that will filter out the creepy-crawlies.

Well, what the hell. There's a school of thought that says we should all be drinking a glass of urine every day. Gandhi did and lived to a healthful, ripe old age. And even our own scientists will admit that drinking urine probably won't do you any harm.

Who knows? Maybe this is the diet breakthrough we've been waiting for. I know I could lose a few pounds if I was restricted to personally rehydrated US Army rations.

Of course I wouldn't call it the Army Whiz Diet. I'd call it by its proper name.

Fasting.

LAUGH? I THOUGHT I'D DIET

You want to hear my nomination for the deadliest four-word combination in the English language?

"I'm on a diet."

Whenever someone says those words to you, you might as well excuse yourself, go home and pull the blankets over your head. You're definitely not going to have any fun with someone who's "on a diet." They'll be bitchy and out of sorts, and they'll stay that way until they come to their senses, give up the diet and go back to burgers and sundaes.

The sad fact is, so many of our friends *are* on diets nowadays. Someone figured out that at any given time, fifteen percent of the population is trying to lose weight by drastically modifying what they eat. Which means that at any given time, four and a half million fellow Canadians are not eating—and feeling irritable about it.

They've got lots of choices. There's the Atkins Diet. And the Stillman Diet. And the Scarsdale, Pritikin, Drinking Man's, High Protein and Weight Watchers Diet.

Which one works? Every one of 'em—providing you stick to it. And that's the catch: virtually everyone who goes on the diet bandwagon eventually falls off—and usually winds up putting on more weight than they lost.

That is...until now.

Gather around friends, for I bring news of the latest diet fad to come down the pike. With this revolutionary approach you don't have to count calories, figure out protein percentages or worry about whether kumquats qualify as a permissible fruit or a verboten vegetable.

That's because on this diet, you won't be eating any kumquats. Matter of fact, you won't be eating any fruits. Or vegetables.

You won't be eating anything at all.

It's called the Breatharian Diet and the name says it all. On this diet, you subsist on your own breath—air—and that's it, Miss Piggy.

You think I'm making this up, doncha? I'm not. There is a Breatharian Society with headquarters in Brisbane, Australia. Disciples of the society insist that they live exclusively on a diet of air and light—which they call "pranic nourishment." They tell anyone who will listen that through meditation and creative visualization they have "rewired" their bodies so that they no longer require conventional food and drink.

Advantages? Breatharians claim that giving up grub has given them more energy, greater creativity and better sex lives.

Not to mention much lower grocery bills.

Head of the movement is a woman who goes by the name of Jasmuheen. She lives in Brisbane and she's written a book called *Living On Light: A Source of Nutrition for the New Millennium.*

There's a Breatharian Chapter on this side of the water too. It's called the Breatharian Institute of America and it's run by a fellow by the name of Wiley Brooks.

Correction: it used to be run by Mr. Brooks. He had to resign after he was spotted ordering a package of Twinkies at a 7-Eleven store.

As for Jasmuheen, her credibility became somewhat strained after a reporter interviewing her at home peeked into her refrigerator and found it stocked from ice cube tray to crisper with enough vegetarian food to feed an ashram.

Jasmuheen claimed that the food belonged to her partner, Jeff Ferguson, but that didn't add to her trustworthiness much. Not after the reporter dug into Mr. Ferguson's history and discovered he'd been convicted of fraud.

Jasmuheen torpedoed herself again when she invited a journalist to accompany her on a flight from Australia to London. When Jasmuheen got to the desk, the agent asked her in a loud voice to confirm that she had ordered an in-flight vegan meal.

"No, no," she protested, rolling her eyes at the journalist, and then, "Well, yes, okay I did. But I won't be eating it."

Hey, Bill Clinton could relate to that. He smoked pot—but didn't inhale.

The bottom line is that Breatharianism is a crock, a con and a farce. Anyone who knows anything about nutrition will tell you—hell, your own common sense will tell you—that the human body cannot live on a diet of air and light.

"If you just laid in bed," says one expert, "you'd probably be okay for about a week. But then your blood would thicken, your kidneys would back up and fail, followed by every other organ in your body and you would die."

Tragically, some naifs have taken the "philosophy" of Breatharianism seriously. One was found in her tent in the Scottish Highlands, expired but still clutching a copy of Jasmuheen's book. Last summer, a thirty-three-year-old Australian voluntarily put herself on the Breatharian diet. She died in a Brisbane hospital. The bizarre doctrine has also been blamed for the death of a German kindergarten teacher.

Mind you...they all lost quite a bit of weight before they went.

WHAT'S YOUR PHOBIA?

For my money, the best interview question ever asked came from Oriana Fallaci at a NASA press conference in Florida more than thirty years ago. The feisty Italian journalist was covering the return of the Apollo 11 space flight on which Neil Armstrong and company became the first humans ever to plant a boot on another planet. Fallaci, a wee mite of a thing, was almost trampled by the hordes of big-shouldered, slavering male reporters who peppered the astronauts with abstruse, technical questions about G-forces, oxygen ratios, orbital fluctuations and the like. The astronauts responded with answers that could have come from well-programmed robots. Finally the moderator noticed Fallaci's waving hand. "Yes," he said, "the Italian reporter…you have a question?"

And Fallaci, all five feet nothing of her, stood up and asked the astronauts: "Were you *scared?*"

It was the question we all wanted to know the answer to. Only Fallaci had the wit to ask it.

Ironically the astronauts' reaction to the question was…fearful. They were off their turf. Out of their comfort zone. It made them one of us again. I would guess the fear that engulfed the astronauts at that moment was topophobia—fear of performing. We can all relate to that.

Fear is the primordial electric current that hard-wires us all. As a matter of fact, I had a grandmother who was electrophobic. She was convinced electricity was seeping out of the wall sockets and pooling dangerously on the carpets.

I myself was clinophobic as a child—terrified of going to bed. That's because of the alligator I was certain lived under my cot.

Most of us are at least mildly brontophobic—we get a little apprehensive when we find ourselves in the middle of a thunder and lightning storm. And I venture to guess the planet is currently undergoing a virtual epidemic of cyberphobia—fear of computers.

A lot of well-known folks have lugged phobias around on their backs. Famous nutbar Howard Hughes suffered from a fear of public places (agoraphobia) and a fear of germs (mysophobia). Canadian comic David Steinberg is deathly afraid of snakes (ophidophobia), while Malcolm Lowry, the novelist, suffered from pnigophobia—a fear of choking on fish bones. I wonder what Lowry ate during the fifteen years he spent living in a shack on a beach north of Vancouver? I sure hope he didn't suffer from arachibutyrphobia (fear of peanut butter sticking to the roof of your mouth).

The worst kinds of phobia are the ones that inspire ridicule in others. How can we accept with a straight face that comedian Sid Caesar suffered from acute tonsurophobia—fear of haircuts? Or that Queen Elizabeth I of Britain was anthophobic—terrified of roses?

So what do you do to combat your phobia—check into a hospital? Not if you're iatrophobic, i.e. frightened of doctors. Decisions, decisions. It's enough to turn one into a raving decidophobic (a person incapable of coming to conclusions).

Sometimes the gods who bestow phobias exhibit a rich sense of irony. Toward the end of his life, billionaire philanthropist Andrew Carnegie developed chrometophobia, the fear of money. The sight of even a dollar bill alarmed and nauseated him and he refused to carry any cash. Richie Valens had all the money and fame a rock 'n' roller could handle, but he also had a crushing case of aerophobia—fear of flying. He died in a plane crash in 1959. The only thing that really frightened actress Natalie Wood was deep water (aquaphobia). She drowned off Santa Catalina Island in 1981.

Then there's the phobia that even the best hotels acknowledge. Ever wondered why North America high rises almost always skip from the twelfth to the fourteenth floor? Triskaidekaphobia—fear of the number thirteen. It's a fear that Romanian labourer Florin Carcu could relate to because he had a bad case of it. Carcu's fear was so strong that last summer, on the morning of Friday, August 13 he phoned his boss begging for the day off. "It was the strangest request," says his boss, "but I ended up giving him permission to stay home. He seemed to be really scared of something bad happening to him that day."

Carcu should have taken his chances at work. He died from a wasp sting while making himself a cup of coffee in his kitchen.

ELVIS A SCOT? GUDE LAIRD!

To paraphrase the late, great Friendly Giant, I want you, dear reader, to look up, waaaaaay up. All the way up to the tippy-top northeast corner of Scotland, there to espy the wee village of Lonmay, not far from Aberdeen.

Okay? Now I want you to look back, waaaaaaay back, to the year 1745. See that burly fella with the Popeye forearms heading out of town with all his worldly possessions in a gunnysack and a one-way ticket to North America sticking out of his pocket?

That would be Andy—Andy of Lonmay to his friends. He's emigrating to America—to the American south, in fact—where he will continue his vocation as a blacksmith, gradually sand down his Scottish burr to a Mississippi drawl, and make his seminal (literally) contribution to one of the great legends of the twentieth century.

It's all foretold in the family name Andy is painstakingly printing in block letters for the ship's manifest: "Presley."

You're looking at Andrew Presley—the great-great-great-great-great-great-great-grandfather of Mr. Rock 'n' Roll, Elvis Aron Presley.

At least that's the way Alan Morrison figures it. He's written a book called *The Presley Prophecy* and he claims he's traced Elvis's roots back eight generations—right to August 27, 1713, when the father of the aforementioned Andrew Presley tied the knot with one Elspeth Leg in Lonmay, Scotland.

Elspeth? Sounds like someone with a lisp trying to say "Elvis" does it nae?

If Morrison is right, that means Elvis's blood type is indisputably tartan.

Elvis a Scot. Gude Laird, have we not done enough damage? Scots have already given the world plaid, curling, oatmeal, Argyle socks, haggis, kilts and bagpipes. Will the abuse never end?

Blasphemy, you cry? Nonsense. I speak as a descendant of a long line of lowland sheep molesters. The "Blacks" whose name I carry were members of an obscure sect of the MacGregor clan. Why "Black?" Who knows? Maybe some of my ancestors were blacksmiths like Andy Presley. Or perhaps we specialized in chimney sweeping. Possibly we were a band of rogues whose full name was Blacksheep. Or it could be we just practised spectacularly poor personal hygiene—I don't know. It doesn't matter. Even though I am almost as far removed from the heather-clad hills as the King himself, my lineage is undeniable. I am—och, aye—a Scot.

The genealogical evidence may be lacking but I can feel it in my bones. I actually like porridge, for God's sake. I watched the Briar last winter. And the slightest skirl of the bagpipes sends a tingle through my carcass, closely followed by the insane desire to mount a suicidal charge—if not on a German machine gun nest, at least upon the tone-deaf hell hound playing the pipes. Only a descendant of the inmates on the far side of Hadrian's Wall could betray such a chequered pedigree.

Of course, I jest—and that's Scottish too. In this alum-sphinctered, hyper-politically correct world we live in, it would be worth my life to make such ethnically disparaging jokes about Muslims, Italians, Comanches, Bosnians, Nigerians or Québécois—but jokes about Scots? Hey, take your best shot. We are the human piñatas of stand-up comedy. The last ethnic group you can safely laugh at.

Why? Because we can take it. My people are as obstinate as Scotch broom, as sturdy as Scotch pine, as hearty as Scotch broth and as tenacious as Scotch tape.

We are also reputed to be somewhat on the thrifty side. I can't confirm or deny the charge, but I will relate the tale of my great-uncle Harry and his visit to London some years ago. Uncle Harry got on a city bus, tucked his suitcase under the seat and said to the conductor, "Tower of London, please."

"That'll be 60p plus 10p for the suitcase," said the conductor.

"What?" said Uncle Harry. "I'll no pay for my suitcase!"

"If you don't pay for the suitcase," said the conductor, "I'll throw it off the bus."

Uncle Harry refused. The conductor picked up the suitcase and pitched it straight out the door—right into the River Thames.

Uncle Harry was outraged. "You English crook!" he roared. "You're not satisfied with trying to rob me, you're trying to drown my wee lad as well!"

EYE OF NEWT AND TOE OF FROG

Well, I ain't superstitious,
But a black cat crossed my trail...
Willie Dixon

Well, I ain't superstitious either. We live in the twenty-first century, after all. We've put a man on the moon, a woman (albeit for a nanosecond) in 24 Sussex Drive and candy stripes in our toothpaste. We're sophisticated, well-rounded, rational people here on Spaceship Earth. It's high time we divested ourselves of medieval old wives' tales about bad-luck cats, bloodsucking bats, headless horsemen, wart-dispensing frogs and other long-leggity beasties that supposedly go bump in the night.

Not that a few superstitions don't make a certain amount of sense. It is merely prudent to avoid walking under a ladder and it's a good idea to let sleeping dogs lie. But some of the other stuff people believe!

You want a sure-fire cure for whooping cough? Cozy up to the nearest nag you can find and inhale a few whiffs of horse's breath.

Know how to cleanse a sickroom of "enfeebled spirits?" Open the window and invite in a cloud of gnats.

Would you like to improve your luck? Catch yourself a well-speckled ladybug. The number of spots on the beetle's back equals the number of "lucky months" you've got coming to you.

It's all very silly and primitive of course—about as silly and primitive as the ancient practice of "bleeding" a patient to release foul humours.

Actually, ahem, it seems the ancients might have been onto something there. Doctors in Britain—and a few here in North America—are enthusiastically slapping slimy bloodsucking leeches on the carcasses of plastic surgery patients these days. It appears the leech's saliva contains an enzyme that acts as an anticoagulant and cuts down the chance of infection.

There's something even creepier that you can get by prescription at the Princess of Wales Hospital in Bridgend, Wales: maggots. Doctors there have found that a generous dollop of live, wriggling maggots on an infected wound can work healing wonders that regular drugs can't touch. Apparently, maggots eat only diseased flesh and bacteria, leaving healthy tissue alone. This is, believe it or not, an improvement on the usual shoot-em-up-with-a-dose-of-antibiotics treatment. Bacteria routinely develop immunity to antibiotics, but they're no match for a platoon of hungry maggots. What's more the maggots are, well, dirt-cheap, easy to transport and generally get the job done within three days.

Oh, yes, and vampire bats? Turns out they're actually good for us too—indirectly. Medical researchers have managed to genetically engineer a new drug they call desmoteplase. It is remarkably effective in restoring normal functions to stroke victims, even when administered as much as nine hours after an attack. Want to guess where they found the model for desmoteplase?

In the saliva of a vampire bat.

It's funny how we rely on animals to bail us out—in superstition and in fact. Sounds kind of grotesque nowadays, but when I was a kid, just about all the people I knew had a rabbit's foot attached to their key chains. It was supposed to bring good luck. Another thing that was supposed to keep the rain off your parade was a horseshoe nailed over your doorway. A visitor to the country cottage of Nobel prizewinner Niels Bohr was astounded to find that even the eminent Danish physicist had a horseshoe over his cottage entrance. "Can it be that you, of all people, believe a horseshoe will bring you luck?" he was asked.

"Of course not," replied Bohr, "but I understand it brings you luck whether you believe in it or not."

The great Italian tenor Enrico Caruso was intensely superstitious. He refused to travel on Fridays. He insisted on slipping a coin into his right-hand pocket before putting on a new pair of pants.

And to protect his golden voice from his habit of smoking sixty cigarettes a day, Caruso wore a necklace from which a dried anchovy was suspended.

Caruso died from abscessed lungs at the age of forty-eight.

Small wonder. There's only so much a dried anchovy can do for a guy.

IT'S A FATHEAD'S WORLD

You know what Hollywood stars have that separates them from the rest of us?

Big heads.

I don't mean big egos, though Lord knows they often have those too—I'm talking about literally big...heads. Take Vanna White, the famous letter turner on the TV show *Wheel of Fortune*. You know why producer Merv Griffin picked her out of a mob of hopefuls? It wasn't her blonde hair, her winning smile or her twin ahems that landed her the job. Neither was it her dexterity at flipping large pieces of cardboard while smiling inanely.

"The truth is," says Griffin, "what made me choose her photo over all the others is that Vanna has a large head." Griffin claims oversized noggins exaggerate an actor's features and make them look striking on camera.

I don't know if all Hollywood marquee types have big heads but I know it applies to Tommy Lee Jones. On screen Jones has a very arresting presence; it's hard to take your eyes off him. But I saw him coming out of a restaurant once and his head is huge! In person he looks like a pumpkin on a stick.

So a big head might land you a gig in La-La Land—but does it indicate that there's extra grey matter inside? Are people with basketball-sized beans any smarter than the average bear?

Actually, yes. According to a study put out by the Environmental Epidemiology Unit in Southampton, England, being born with a big head is a bit like winning the genetic lottery. The study found that babies with high birth weights (which, they say, invariably means babies with big heads)—developed better reading skills, superior reasoning and more reliable memories.

What's more, the benefits keep on coming, right into old age. Senior citizens with large heads consistently suffer less mental decline than pinheads like you and me.

But cheer up. Just because the übernoggins have more brainpower doesn't mean they're a lap ahead in the evolutionary race. Scientists at the University of Fribourg in Switzerland managed to selectively breed a group of fast-learning fruit flies—in other words, smarter-than-your-average-fruit-fly fruit flies. They then pitted these A-student bugs against a flock of dull-average fruit flies in a contest for scarce food.

The brainy bugs got fat while the dumb ones went hungry, right?

Exactly wrong. The dullard flies thrived while the superflies just sat around and starved. The researchers concluded that the so-called superior fruit flies were literally too smart for their own good. They spent too much of their energy making connections among the neurons in their brains, which left them less energy to forage for food.

Being smart doesn't guarantee success—for fruit flies or for humans. If being smart was all it took to flourish as a species, we'd all be wearing laurel wreaths and conversing in ancient Greek. The world would be looking up to leaders like Plato and Aristotle.

Instead we get Governor Schwarzenegger and George Dubya.

But if you're feeling you got shortchanged in the upper-story sweepstakes, cheer up. These are only scientific studies, after all. That means that they are subject to the frailties and myopia of the boffins who set them up.

Scientists are famous for failing to identify forests because of all the damn trees that get in their line of sight.

Like the Russian biologist who trained a flea to jump by verbal command. "Jump!" said the scientist. The flea jumped.

The scientist removed one front leg and told the flea to jump again.

It did. The scientist recorded, "Upon removal of one leg, all flea organs function properly."

Next, he removed one back leg. Still the flea could jump on command. The scientist dutifully noted, "Upon removal of second leg, all flea organs function properly."

He then removed all of the flea's legs and commanded, "Jump!"

Nothing happened.

Whereupon the scientist recorded, "Upon removal of last leg, the flea loses its sense of hearing."

GAMES PEOPLE PLAY

Don't get me wrong, I like Frankie. I meet him downtown a couple of times a week for a coffee and we have good chats...sorta. The truth is, Frankie is a bit of a wet blanket. The original Eeyore. His name should really be Gus. As in Gloomy.

Yesterday I hauled up a stool next to him at the coffee shop, gritted my teeth, forced my lips into a rictus smile and said with as much enthusiasm as I could muster, "How's it goin', Frankie?"

"Oh, same old, same old," he moans. "There's nothing to do in this town."

Well, I snapped. Came undone. Went postal.

"Nothing to do?" I shrieked. "Whaddya mean there's nothing to do? Have you thought of seeing how many somersaults you can do between here and Fulford Harbour? How about lashing a rope to the bumper of a fire truck and seeing how far you can pull it? Or if it's a cardiovascular workout you want, why not pogo-stick up the inside stairwell of the CN Tower?"

Frankie was getting nervous now, edging toward the exit. "Yeah," he said, "those are all...really good ideas. Well, look at the time, willya. I gotta go."

Frankie thinks I'm nuts, but in fact I was just reciting some of the routine ploys people have performed to get their names in the latest edition of the *Guinness Book of Records.*

The Reverend Kevin Fast (five foot nine, 270 pounds) of Cobourg, Ontario, is in there for pulling a thirty-ton Goliath fire truck a hundred feet using only a rope. And a New York health-food store manager by the name of Ashrita Furman is the guy who pogo-sticked up the CN Tower stairwell AND somersaulted continuously for a distance of twelve miles, 390 yards.

Truth to tell, Furman is a record-setting legend. In fact he holds the Guinness record for being in the *Guinness Book of Records*—seventy-two entries in total, all of them mind-boggling.

It's amazing what some people will do to get attention—and it's not always a slot in the *Guinness Book of Records* they're after. A couple of months ago, a British artist by the name of Mark McGowan wanted to bring public attention to the problem of student debt. Did he write a letter to the editor? No. Did he don a sandwich board and picket the Ministry of Education offices? No. Did he strip down to his skivvies and call a press conference? No. What he did is roll a peanut from his studio in southeast London all the way to the front door at Number 10 Downing Street.

With his nose.

McGowan spent eight hours a day and most of the month of September schnozz-bunting his peanut along the sidewalks of London. When he got there McGowan handed the (other) nut over to an official along with a letter asking Prime Minister Tony Blair to accept it as payment in full for his student loan.

Yeah, that should work, Mark.

Sometimes the inspiration for oddball pranks is decidedly spiritual. A Buddhist priest in Japan by the name of Genshin Fujinami has spent three months (actually, a hundred consecutive days) of each of the past seven years rising at midnight and running eighteen miles, pausing 250 times along the way to pray. And no Lycra bodysuits and Nike runners for this marathon monk—he did it wearing only a robe and straw sandals. Total distance covered in seven years: 24,800 miles.

Fujinami's ordeal is, believe it or not, a Japanese tradition dating back to 1885. In the past century and a bit, hundreds of monks have tried to duplicate Fujinami's feat. Only forty-six have made it.

What is it that drives people to such behavioural extremes? A craving for fame in many cases—but not always. Ashrita Furman, the dean of goofy gambits, says, "The Guinness Records are silly in and of themselves, but they give me an opportunity to meditate and learn things about myself, about endurance."

They can also teach you the importance of doing your homework. Last month, a Californian by the name of Jim Hager set a world record for eating M&M candies with chopsticks. He picked off 115 of the slithery little goodies in three minutes.

Alas, the judges at Guinness Records disqualified Hager. The original record had been set with Smarties.

HAIR TODAY AND GONE TOMORROW

...the law, sir, is a ass—a idiot.

If anyone needed visual confirmation of the words Charles Dickens put in the mouth of Mr. Bumble, one need go no farther than a typical British courtroom during a typical British trial. There you might watch one of Britain's most eminent barristers mellifluously declaiming subtle and abstruse points of law in soaring language with Shakespearean flourishes and Miltonian profundity.

And he will be dressed like a geriatric drag queen.

British barristers wear robes and wigs. Have done since the seventeenth century. And I don't mean understated Frank Sinatra hairpieces or sleek Captain Kirk toupées—the wigs the Brits wear are mangy, white pageboy bobs, made out of horse hair, crudely cut, heavily powdered and heavy as sin.

Sure, they made a dynamite fashion statement back in the sixteen hundreds, but nowadays—why? Traditionalists argue that the wigs and robes help instill respect for the law.

Yeah, right—but why not go for something lighter and more contemporary, like Groucho Marx glasses and a Ronald McDonald clown suit?

Ah, well. Men have always been a little loony in the head hair department. I haven't got as much mileage (or hair) as Rumpole of the

Bailey, but I've lived through brush cuts, boogie cuts, Elvis pompadours, ducktails, Afros, Beatle cuts, Mohawks, buzz cuts and the Mel Gibson mullet.

I don't want to come on like I'm cutting-edge trendy when it comes to hair, but—well, I *am* cue-ball bald. And that, my friends, is the latest hot look for gents—no hair at all.

And not just on the head. Have you seen Arm & Hammer's latest cosmetic come-on? Nair For Men.

The male-targeted hair removal gel has been selling briskly down south for a while now. According to a survey released by the company that manufactures the stuff, thirty percent of American males between the ages of eighteen and thirty-four regularly shave off their chest hair.

When did this start? I thought the hairy-chested he-man was the standard all ninety-pound-weaklings aspired to.

Ah, but that was before Ah-nold. As a body-builder, Governor Conan proved that you could have a chest as bare as a baby's bum and still look like a walking bag of walnuts.

According to scientists, Schwartzetcetra and his hair-removing imitators may simply be responding to a biological imperative. Researchers at Oxford and Reading universities suggest we humans originally shed our furry primate pelts half a million years ago to protect ourselves from disease-carrying parasites.

"Smooth skin has therefore become an evolutionary calling card we use unconsciously to pick healthy mates," says Sir Walter Bodner, an Oxford University spokesman.

Admittedly, those guys you see at the beach in thongs and what looks like a welcome mat growing on their backs probably aren't sexual turn-ons for anybody this side of a lowland gorilla in heat. Still I think I'll cling to what's left of my body hair.

My beard, I mean—particularly after what happened to my pal Arvid. He was down at the local barbershop getting a shave last week and he mentioned the trouble he has getting a smooth shave around the cheeks.

"Got just the thing," said the barber, taking a small wooden ball from a nearby drawer. "Before you shave, just put this in your mouth between your cheek and your gum."

So Arvid tries it. He pops the ball in his mouth, it makes his cheek puff out, and sure enough—the barber proceeds to give him the closest, smoothest shave he's ever experienced.

"This ib grape, Al," says Arvid, trying to talk around the ball, "but what happens if I swallow it?"

"No problem," says the barber. "Just bring it back tomorrow like everyone else does."

THE MADNESS OF KING GEORGE

Not to be paranoid or anything, but what if it turns out that George Dubya is actually certifiably nuts?

I don't mean eccentric, bipolar, idiosyncratic or just plain dopey. I mean flat out, bouncing off the walls, call-for-the-guys-in-white-coats wacko.

It's not unheard of historically—even among leaders named George. Britain's King George III became a raving loony just a few years into his reign back in the eighteenth century. He died decades later, blind, deaf and mad—but still king.

Then there was Charles VI of France, who threw a royal ball at which he had his courtiers dress up as "savages" with feathers glued to their skins. Charles then encouraged them to toss blazing torches at one another. Not surprisingly this caused the feathers and other costumes to catch fire. Six guests at the ball burned to death.

Charles VI was also known as Charles the Mad.

Nor did the Germans get off lightly in the royal nutbar department. Maximilian II of Bavaria never smiled from boyhood to the day of his death at the age of fifty-three. His son Ludwig II believed Marie Antoinette was the reincarnation of the Virgin Mary and ate his meals at a table that was really an elevator. It could be lowered one floor into the kitchen so that empty dishes could be removed and the next course added on. That way Ludwig didn't have to see his servants.

He may also have been avoiding brother Otto, who barked like a dog and once refused to take off his boots. For eight weeks.

We won't even mention the British royal family.

Delusionary behaviour is not unknown on this continent either. Who can forget Stockwell (call me Doris) Day, and his confident assertion that cavemen and dinosaurs cohabited on an earth that is really only six thousand years old? Mr. Day, thankfully, did a career-ending face-plant while lurching toward 24 Sussex Drive. Not like Mackenzie King, Canada's tenth prime minister. King regularly sought political advice from his dog, Leonardo da Vinci and his mother, who—like Leonardo—happened to be dead at the time.

As for presidential precedents, well, Ronald Reagan once regaled Israeli Prime Minister Yitzhak Shamir with tales of how he helped liberate Auschwitz. Only trouble is, Reagan never got closer to World War II than a couple of training films he cranked out in Hollywood. Reagan thought of himself as a war hero. He never saw a day of combat.

That's kinda crazy.

Richard Nixon may not have been certifiable, but he was definitely intellectually compromised from time to time. Recently released transcripts of 1970s White House phone calls reveal Secretary of State Henry Kissinger running desperate interference for the commander-in-chief. On the very brink of the Arab-Israeli war the British prime minister could not reach the Oval Office. That's because Kissinger had the telephone off the hook, explaining, as we can hear on the transcript, "When I talked to the president, he was loaded."

And George W.? The man who has publicly declared he believes "God wanted me to be president?" Well, Carolyn Williams, a psychoanalyst who specializes in paranoia (and is also a card-carrying Republican, by the bye), says, "His behaviour does suggest a classic paranoid personality."

Dr. Justin Frank, author of *Bush on the Couch: Inside the Mind of the President,* goes further than that. He diagnoses Bush as "an untreated ex-alcoholic with paranoid and megalomaniacal tendencies." He also suggests that Bush's belligerent behaviour may stem from an unconscious resentment of men and women in the American armed forces "whose bravery puts his own [non-existent] wartime service record to shame."

Well, I dunno about that. But I read in a recent issue of *Time* magazine that President Bush's favourite Oval Office show-off memento these days is the pearl-handled automatic that was taken from Saddam Hussein when he was captured. The GIs who arrested Hussein had the gun mounted and presented to Bush. "He really likes showing it off," says one recent visitor.

Bush keeps the handgun in his study. The same study where former president Bill Clinton shared cigars with Monica Lewinsky.

Not to be paranoid or anything…

LONG LIVE THE TABS

Lord knows there's an Everglades worth of strange and weirdling places in the state of Florida, but few more so than a veritable Twilight Zone near the town of Lantana known as Tabloid Valley. This is where, believe it or not, most of the lurid scandal sheets that grace supermarket checkout counters across North America come from (it must be some kind of tax dodge). The *National Enquirer* comes out of Tabloid Valley. So does the *Weekly World News.*

Or at least it did. It's hard to say what will become of the *Weekly World News* now that Eddie Clontz is dead.

Clontz was editor-in-chief of the *Weekly World News* for nearly twenty years. He's the guy responsible for the Elvis-never-died stories. He also had a hand in such classic exclusives as "Space Aliens Back Bush for President" and "Bat Boy Found in West Virginia Cave."

I met Eddie Clontz in the offices of the *Weekly World News* about ten years ago. But it wasn't easy. I wanted to interview Clontz for my radio show, so I asked one of my old pals, an ex-tab reporter by the name of Harold Fiske, the best way to go about it. "Good luck!" said Fiske. Clontz, he told me, was a reclusive and deeply suspicious guy. Rumour had it that he kept a pearl-handled .45 automatic in the top drawer of his desk. Reason? Death threats. From diehard Elvis fans, mostly.

For a hard-nosed, foot-in-the-door newshound, Harold Fiske could be incredibly ingratiating. Over the next few days he called in some favours, twisted a few arms, greased a palm or two, and the next thing I knew we were in a Hertz rent-a-car bombing down the I-95 for a face-to-face with Eddie Clontz.

The offices of the *Weekly World News* are deep in the middle of the Florida boonies and at first glance seem utterly devoid of human life. There is no secretary or doorman or security guard in sight. What there is is a closed-circuit camera mounted over a locked door with an intercom on the side. I thumbed the talkback button, leaned into the intercom and said, "Arthur Black here to interview Mr. Clontz."

"STAND AWAY FROM THE DOOR!" said a large voice which I presumed to be God's. Befuddled, I stood there stupidly and repeated my mantra. The voice became noticeably agitated: "SIR! STAND AWAY FROM THE DOOR! NOW!" I backed up, raised my hands in the air and smiled weakly. I guess I convinced them that I wasn't a vengeance-bent Elvis fan because the door hissed open and suddenly I was in the air-conditioned inner sanctum of the *Weekly World News.*

I don't know what I expected—a bunch of grimy, boil-blighted trolls scuttling around with cigar butts sticking out of their mouths, maybe—but it wasn't like that at all. The office was clean and neat, the equipment was state-of-the-art, the desks were tidy and the people were well-dressed and exceedingly normal-looking. Hell, it looked like a Brandon branch office of Mutual of Omaha.

Except for Eddie Clontz. There was no mistaking Eddie, or the fact that he was in charge. He was middle-aged but fit, like a retired NHLer. He had a brush cut and black button eyes that never blinked. His desk sat so that he faced the office door, and I couldn't help noticing that his hands stayed close to the top desk drawer. If I had been a demented reader bent on violence, Eddie could've plugged me before I got to his inbox.

I was disabused of a lot of my tabloid notions that afternoon. I learned that the tabs, despite their surface sleaziness, are as cunningly thought out, written and published as any edition of the *New York Review of Books.* I learned that tabloid reporters are not rabid, red-eyed right-wingers or raving alcoholics riding out the nether end of a death-spiralling career. Most of them are young and bright and surprisingly serious. They need to be, because writing even a mediocre tabloid story is fiendishly difficult. You have to deliver a maximum amount of impact with a minimal number of words—and simple words at that.

And nobody ever wanted to pass a mediocre story across Eddie Clontz's desk. Especially if he was sitting at it, with his hands near the top drawer.

Tabloids. The word originally referred to medicine delivered in tablet form. As a reporter for the *Weekly World News* once said, "Readers want new hope. They want to think that UFOs will save us. It's medicine. We make people feel good, so they buy us."

Hmm. All I know is, the headlines in my *Globe and Mail* are all about scandal in Ottawa, soaring prices at the gas pump, and body bags in Iraq.

A wise woman once said, "The news is a disease that masquerades as information."

Call me escapist, but I think I'd rather read about the latest Elvis sighting.

IDEAS: DUMB AND OTHERWISE

I know a guy who once dived into a dumpster full of pig manure and came up with an apple in his mouth. It was a publicity stunt for some jock-rock radio station and he actually got paid for it.

I don't know how much, but it wasn't enough.

Dumb idea? No question. But there are a lot of dumb ideas out there. George Bush's missile defence initiative is a colossally dumb idea. As is Donald Trump's notion of tonsorial splendour.

But then so is Karl-Friedrich Lentze's straight banana proposition. Herr Lentze is a German inventor currently seeking a patent for what he calls the "cigar-banana." Lentze's theory: the traditional curved banana is a freak of nature calling out for rational modification. His patent application envisions an assembly line on which an endless chain of bananas would have their curvy midsections mechanically excised after which the top and bottom sections of the fruit would be hermetically joined using what Lentze calls a "biologically safe plaster." And the curvy culls? Lentze says they wouldn't be wasted. They'd be diverted and sold for use in "fruit salads and things like that."

Lentze thinks the cigar-banana is, as the cliché goes, an idea whose time has come. "Once people get used to them I believe the cigar-banana will drive the curved banana from the market. It's easier to eat and easier to store."

No offence, Karl-Friedrich, but...dumb idea. If any food ever gets easier to eat than a banana—curved, straight or tied in a Windsor knot—I want to be there with my own patent application.

Speaking of dumb ideas—what do you make of Danny Wallace? You heard of his dumb idea? A couple of years ago he calls up the advertising department of a small magazine in London, England, to place an ad. Content of the ad? Just two words—"Join me"—followed by a request to send a small passport photo.

That was it! No context. No explanation. The folks in the advertising department figured Wallace was bonkers, but he gave them a valid credit card number so they ran the ad.

At last count, nine thousand people had responded.

And not just Flat-Earthers, JFK conspiracists and folks who believe Elvis is alive and pumping gas in Topeka, Kansas. British Prime Minister Tony Blair sent a message of support. So did Prince Charles. Last April, Wallace got a plane ticket in the mail along with an invitation to address the international Philanthropy Workshop in Geneva. This is an ultra-conservative think-tank bankrolled by the US Rockefeller Foundation and the German Bertelsmann Foundation. Eight of the most influential men in the world—billionaires all—assembled and listened intently as Danny Wallace outlined his ideas.

And what precisely are his ideas—aside from the spooky imperative "Join me?"

Hard to say. Nobody from the billionaire summit is talking (they're sworn to secrecy) and Danny Wallace is cryptic at the best of times. But if I read it right, the Join Me movement breaks down into a philosophy of another two words: be kind.

One of his initiatives took the form of a commandment that he sent out to all nine thousand "joinees." It read "Make an old man happy." His disciples sprang into action performing spontaneous acts of kindness to geezer guys everywhere and sending back photographic proof to Wallace's mailing address.

But then he figured, "Why just old men?" And so another suggestion went out asking his disciples to "commit random acts of kindness" to people of either sex and any age every Friday. He calls this the Good Friday agreement.

The story of Join Me spread across the channel, first to Belgium, then throughout Western Europe. Last March, Danny Wallace did a tour of the US to talk about Join Me.

So exactly who profits from this movement? Well, here's what Danny Wallace says: "If you asked me a year ago who I thought would benefit most from these random acts of kindness, I'd have said the recipients. Now I'm pretty sure it's fifty-fifty. Thanks to these small and happy efforts I've watched people come out of their shells, shed their embarrassment, make new friends. I've watched people become the people they've always known they were but were too shy to show. I've watched people glow as they made someone else smile.

"Try it. You'll see what I mean."

Hmm. Perhaps a dumb idea whose time has come?

www.joinme.co.uk

NAVEL INTELLIGENCE

Did I ever mention how much I love to get letters from readers? Your letters invariably cheer me up—except when they threaten to tear out my tongue and use it for a necktie, but that's a rarity. Mostly the letters I get from readers are delightful. I mean, how could it not make my day to receive a letter like this one:

> *Hi, Arthur, how's it going? My husband Andrew and I met you last year at the famous Rolla Pub located in the metropolis of Rolla, BC, when you were the guest of the Purple Donuts. Recently, my husband and I were embroiled in a passionate debate on belly button lint, or more specifically, why men get belly button lint, but women do not. We decided that this was a question right up your alley. Please help end the belly button lint debate. Any information on this topic would be appreciated.*
> Michelle Blair
> Rolla, BC

Well, Michelle, we here at Weird Query Central do what we can. I have to tell you right off that exhaustive research conducted on my own carcass, not to mention those friends who are still speaking to me, reveals no quantifiable gender split when it comes to belly button lint. As near as I can tell, women are not belly button lint deprived.

But your question raised still more questions. Questions like: where does b.b. lint come from? Why is b.b. lint always some shade of blue? Do people with outie belly buttons collect the stuff—or is it only people with innies?

And how come Alfred Hitchcock didn't have either?

What I found was, nobody knows for certain where belly button lint comes from, but betting people usually put their money on the clothing we wear. Their theory is that the stuff rubs off our clothes onto our skin and collects in the nearest pothole—which as often as not is the *omphalos*. (That's the twenty-five-cent word for belly button. You can also use "umbilicus" or the five-cent "navel.") As to why it's so often blue, again the experts suggest that we check the lint screen in our clothes dryers—isn't the lint in there some shade of blue, more often than not? It's just common sense that outies don't get near as much belly button lint as innies—gravity rules! And Hitch didn't have a belly button because it got plowed under and stitched over during some major abdominal surgery.

Speaking of folks with no navels, did you know that Michelangelo nearly got himself drawn and quartered for his portrayal of Adam on the ceiling of the Sistine Chapel? He was the first painter in history to give the guy a belly button! Which was rankest heresy, because Adam was the first human being, right? To whom could he possibly have been umbilical-ed?

The portrayal gave rise to a huge theosophical debate that became known derisively as "Adam's indention and God's intention." It was still raging four hundred years after Michelangelo's death when, during World War II, a US congressional committee refused to okay an instructional booklet for US troops. The committee was worried the booklet would "sap troop morale" because it contained an illustration depicting Adam and Eve with navels.

The horror. The horror.

On the bright side, I am pleased to be able to tell Michelle and all other belly button obsessives that it is now possible to order one hundred percent pure, virgin human belly button lint on the internet.

Why would you want to do that? Well, it's great for starting fires, cleaning guns, and—for purist fishermen—fly tying, to name just a few good reasons. Simply type "virgin belly button lint" into your browser and you're on your way to becoming a proud owner of pristine umbilicus jetsam.

And remember no animals, forests, rivers, oceans or Third World factory workers were exploited in the production of this product. Belly button lint is a guilt-free purchase.

Hey, don't thank me. Just keep those cards and letters coming.

OTHER GREAT BOOKS FROM HARBOUR PUBLISHING

BLACK & WHITE AND READ ALL OVER

Arthur Black

Like a well-delivered punchline, the tenth book by award-winning writer Arthur Black is guaranteed to make you laugh.

ISBN 1-55017-336-7 • 6 x 9 • 272 pages

FLASH BLACK

Arthur Black

The author of *Black Tie and Tales* and *Black in the Saddle Again*, both winners of the Stephen Leacock Medal for Humour, returns with a new collection guaranteed to tickle your funny bone and make you scratch your head at the absurdities of life in the early years of the new millennium. *ISBN 1-55017-330-8 • 6 x 9 • 212 pages*

WHEN NATURE CALLS

Life at a Gulf Islands Cottage

Eric Nicol

A wryly funny, sharply observed book on the joys and terrors of cottage life on Saturna Island in BC's Strait of Georgia, by one of Canada's most beloved humourists. *ISBN 1-55017-210-7 • 6 x 9 • 198 pages*

GRIZZLIES & WHITE GUYS

The Stories of Clayton Mack

Compiled and Edited by Harvey Thommasen

"A drama spattered with blood and craziness...rousingly funny... solid, no-nonsense hunting stories, with all pretense and decoration stripped away."—Tony Eberts, *Vancouver Province.*

ISBN 1-55017-140-2 • 6 x 9 • 30 drawings & photos • 240 pages

These titles are available at bookstores or from:

HARBOUR PUBLISHING

PO Box 219

Madeira Park, BC V0N 2H0

Toll free order line: 1-800-667-2988

Fax: 604-883-9451 • Email: orders@harbourpublishing.com